"For those who do not already know, this elegant essay will show why Shelby Steele is America's clearest thinker about America's most difficult problem. Braiding family memories with an acute understanding of national policies, he demonstrates what went wrong when whites for their reasons, and blacks for theirs, embraced the idea that white guilt explains blacks' problems and can be the basis of policies for ameliorating them." —George F. Will

"With his characteristic honesty, clarity, and hard-won wisdom, Shelby Steele exposes the social hypocrisies and racial lies that transformed the once-promising post–civil rights era into a period of cultural decadence and mediocrity. We owe Citizen Steele our thanks. On questions of race in America—white guilt, black opportunism—he is our twenty-first-century Socrates: the powerful, lucid, and elegant voice of a refreshingly independent thinker who desires only to see us liberated from sophistry and self-destructive illusions."
—Charles Johnson, author of *Middle Passage*,
National Book Award winner

"There is no writer who deserves black America's allegiance more than Shelby Steele. . . . Steele's writing is a marvel."
—John McWhorter, *National Review*

"Steele makes a passionate case. . . . A hard, critical look at affirmative action, self-serving white liberals, and self-victimizing black leaders." —*Publishers Weekly*

"The cultural analysis of America's loss of moral authority for its exposed racism has resonance today." —*Booklist*

ALSO BY SHELBY STEELE

The Content of Our Character:
A New Vision of Race in America

A Dream Deferred:
The Second Betrayal of Black Freedom in America

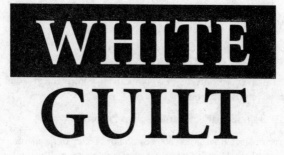

WHITE GUILT

How
Blacks and Whites
Together Destroyed
the Promise of
the Civil Rights Era

SHELBY STEELE

HARPER PERENNIAL

NEW YORK • LONDON • TORONTO • SYDNEY

HARPER PERENNIAL

A hardcover edition of this book was published in 2006 by HarperCollins Publishers.

P.S. ™ is a trademark of HarperCollins Publishers.

HarperCollins books may be purchased for educational, business, or sales promotional use. For information, please e-mail the Special Markets Department at SPsales@harpercollins.com.

FIRST HARPER PERENNIAL EDITION PUBLISHED 2007.

Designed by Nancy Singer Olaguera, ISPN Publishing Services

The Library of Congress has catalogued the hardcover edition as follows:

Steele, Shelby.
    White guilt : how blacks and whites together destroyed the
    promise of the civil rights era / Shelby Steele.—1st ed.
        p. cm.
     ISBN: 978-0-06-057862-6 (acid-free paper)
     ISBN-10: 0-06-057862-9 (acid-free paper)
      1. United States—Race relations. 2. Racism—United States.
    3. African Americans—Politics and government—20th century.
    4. United States—Race relations—Psychological aspects.
    5. Racism—United States—Psychological aspects. I. Title.

E185.615.S7236   2006
305.896'073—dc22   2005052784

ISBN: 978-0-06-057863-3 (pbk.)
ISBN-10: 0-06-057863-7 (pbk.)

 20 21 22 ❖/LSC 20 19 18 17 16 15 14

To Rita, once again

CONTENTS

PART THREE: THE WAYS OF BLINDNESS

PART FOUR: DISSOCIATION AND CULTURE

ACKNOWLEDGMENTS

I would like to thank my editor, Terry Karten, whose discerning responses to early drafts truly helped me make this a better book. I would also like to thank Carol Mann, my agent, who bravely argued for more where more was in fact needed.

I thank the Hoover Institution at Stanford University and its director, John Raisian, not only for continued support but also for the opportunity to try out many of the ideas contained herein on those wonderful and thoughtful Hoover audiences.

PART ONE

THE STORY OF WHITE GUILT

A DILEMMA

Sometimes it is a banality—something a little sad and laughable—that makes you aware of a deep cultural change. On some level you already knew it, so that when the awareness comes, there is more recognition than surprise. Yes, of course, things have changed.

So it was not long after the Clinton-Lewinsky scandal began that it occurred to me that race had dramatically changed the terms by which political power is won and held in America. When I woke on that January morning to the sight of President Clinton wagging his finger on the morning news and saying "I never had sex with that woman," I thought two things: that he was lying and that he would be out of office within two weeks. It was a month later that I realized not only that he might survive his entire term but also that his survival, even for a month, already spoke volumes about the moral criterion for holding power in the United States.

I came to this realization on a drive back to northern

California from Los Angeles with the scandal keeping me company on the car radio. A commentator said that President Eisenhower would not have survived a single day had he been caught in circumstances similar to President Clinton's. Having grown up in the fifties, I thought this was probably true, and this is when the deep cultural shift became clear.

I seemed to remember—in the way that one vaguely remembers gossip about the famous—someone once telling me that Eisenhower occasionally used the word "nigger" on the golf course. Maybe he did; maybe he didn't. In that era we blacks fully assumed that whites in all stations of life used this word at least in private. However, I cannot imagine that a reporter in that era, overhearing Eisenhower speak in this way, would have seen it as anything more than jocular bad taste. Certainly no one would have questioned his fitness to hold office. Yet, if an affair with a young female intern had exploded in the national media, with details of secret retreats off the Oval Office, thongs, cigars, etc., there is little doubt that 1950s America would have judged him morally unfit to hold power. It was taken for granted in that gray-flannel era that public trust had to be reciprocated by a rigorous decorum around sexual matters, even if that decorum was the very face of hypocrisy.

Yet, on that long drive talk-show callers passionately argued that private indiscretions were no bar to public trust, that what Clinton did in his private life had no bearing on his ability to run the country. It was unapologetic moral relativism—the idea that sexual morality is relative only to the consent of the individuals involved, and that there is no other authority or moral code larger than their choice. In the voices of many callers you could hear this expressed as a kind of pride. Relativism spares us from far worse sins, they seemed to be saying, those greatest of all sins for my baby-boomer generation—judgmentalism and hypocrisy.

All this drew me back to my college days in the sixties when we would sit around in the student union, smoking French cigarettes and arguing that monogamy was a passé bourgeois convention. Of course it was an adolescent argument of perfectly transparent wishful thinking, since beneath all the big ideas—at least for us boys—was the fervent hope that the girls would actually believe it. There was a lot of lust in this kind of thinking—lust everywhere in baby-boomer thinking—and over time it became part of the generational license that opened the way for a sexual revolution. But it was jarring these many decades later—so deep now into adult life—to hear such thinking hauled out in defense of the president of the United States.

But then something occurred to me. I wondered if President Clinton would be defended with relativism if he had done what, according to gossip, Eisenhower was said to have done. Suppose that in a light moment he had slipped into a parody of an old Arkansas buddy from childhood and, to get the voice right, used the word "nigger" a few times. Suppose further that a tape of this came to light so that all day long in the media—from the unctuous morning shows to the freewheeling late-night shows to the news every half hour on radio—we would hear the unmistakable presidential voice saying, "Take your average nigger ..."

Today in America there is no moral relativism around racism, no sophisticated public sentiment that recasts racism as a mere quirk of character. Today America is puritanical rather than relativistic around racism, and if Clinton had been caught in this way, it is very likely that nothing would have saved him. The very legitimacy of the American democracy in this post–civil rights era now requires a rigid, if not repressive, morality of racial equality. A contribution of the civil rights movement was to establish the point that a multiracial society cannot be truly democratic unless social equality itself becomes a matter of *personal* morality. So a president's "immorality" in this area would pretty much cancel his legitimacy as a democratic leader.

The point is that President Clinton survived what would certainly have destroyed President Eisenhower, and Eisenhower could easily have survived what would almost certainly have destroyed Clinton. Each man, finally, was no more than indiscreet within the moral landscape of his era (again, Eisenhower's indiscretion is hypothetical here for purposes of discussion). Neither racism in the fifties nor womanizing in the nineties was a profound enough sin to undermine completely the moral authority of a president. So it was the good luck of each president to sin into the moral relativism of his era rather than into its puritanism. And, interestingly, the moral relativism of one era was the puritanism of the other. Race simply replaced sex as the primary focus of America's moral seriousness.

Just out of Los Angeles I decided to set myself the task of exploring this dilemma on the long drive up to Monterey and home. The idea of driving with a mental task was appealing. Maybe the physics of plunging ahead through time and space would give motion and focus to my thoughts. I had been thinking a lot about white guilt just as the Clinton scandal broke. And now I thought this phenomenon might have something to do with the little dilemma I wanted to explore.

But what about form? In the nineteenth century there was a narrative form called the Chautauqua, a kind of narrative lecture through a subject or dilemma that people would listen to for hours, a little longer even than we spend at movies today. There was always an interplay of theme and pertinent digression, and the faith was that digression would bring fuller understanding. Maybe this form would do, with a little of the personal journal thrown in. I could move through two landscapes at the same time—one of coastline, small charming towns, and lush winter-green coastal mountains; the other of memory and thought. All I really needed was something I had already procured: two Starbucks double espressos and a bottled water.

Conventional wisdom says that the America I was driving through on that sunny winter morning had been in moral decline since the sixties—almost everyone's idea of when the American character began its denouement. And there is much evidence to support this wisdom. Since then divorce, illegitimacy, single-parent homes, drug use, and crime have gone up greatly. Marriage rates, levels of academic performance, church attendance, reading, and voting have all gone down. "Declinism" is now a kind of postmodern ideology in certain circles and an academic subject in others.

But something else was also true about America, something that became clear to me as I turned off Highway 101 into San Luis Obispo for a bite to eat. Cruising into the town proper, I experienced what might be called a "segregation flashback." I remembered cruising into another town, decades earlier, on a trip from Chicago to Kentucky with my father to visit relatives. Just off the highway we did what we always did upon entering a new town—what we had to do before any of our personal needs could be met. We went in search of a black person.

Usually we could spot one quickly, but not always, not if we came into town from the white end. Whites were often friendly enough but they had no hard information. Bladder full and stomach empty, it was like finding a treasure to come upon a black person, and my father would swing the car in to the curb, hop out, and in a tone that was at once pleasant and conspiratorial, shout, "Say, chief." In minutes he would be back behind the wheel with a complete local geography of black possibility—houses where we might spend the night (often run by widows), places to eat, and information about churches, taverns, and barbershops. Every black a chamber of commerce unto himself. And then, of course, we would essentially disappear from the white world, where none of these things were available to us, and enter an all-black territory similar to the Chicago-area neighborhood we'd come from.

Now President Eisenhower, along with most white Americans, took a rather relativistic stance toward the segregation that required my family to travel in this way. If he felt it was morally wrong, he nevertheless easily lived with it. He could be, in fact, "sophisticated" about it, "tolerant" of the racist imposition of a segregated existence on blacks and mindful of the need to "go slow" in ending it. He did not want to push Americans (read: whites) away from this immorality too fast.

*   *   *

So, yes, there has been much moral decline in America since the sixties, but it is also true that I drove into San Luis Obispo on that winter morning knowing that I could sleep or eat anywhere my wallet would take me. I had no need to search out a local black person or to find the black part of town. So, in the same decades of America's "moral decline" there had obviously also been a great moral advance. A great evil had been stilled, pushed back, repressed. In downtown San Luis Obispo I searched only for a restaurant that suited me, not one that would have me. And after parking my car, I walked through a world cleansed by a very hard-earned moral advance and held in this new benign state by an unforgiving social puritanism. So it was hard for me, having walked down streets where one's color was a bar to everything, to believe fully in declinism. No doubt the divorce rate in this town is twice what it was when I was unwelcome here. But it is also true that in other ways people here are better than they once were.

Thus, President Clinton's sin was a little anachronistic, a sin against the moral sensibility of another time more than of his own. And this makes the point that the great moral preoccupation and commitment in America today are social. I believe it was our racial history that effectively renormed American culture around social morality. As I was reminded on that morning in San Luis Obispo, there is much good in this. But there is also much bad, much that undermines social equality as surely as racism once did.

But first, how did social morality become ascendant?

2

FIDELITY

The answer begins in the matter of fidelity. In a democracy the legitimacy of institutions and of government itself is earned and sustained through *fidelity* to a discipline of democratic principles. These principles strive to ensure the ennobling conditions that free societies aspire to: freedom for the individual, the same rights for all individuals, equality under the law, equality of opportunity, and an inherent right to "life, liberty, and the pursuit of happiness." Freedom, then, is not a state-imposed vision of the social good (say, a classless society); rather, it is the absence of any imposed vision that would infringe on the rights and freedom of individuals. In a true democracy freedom is a higher priority than the social good.

So freedom is what *follows* from a discipline of principles—equal treatment under the law, one man one vote, freedom of speech, separation of church and state, the litany of individual rights, and so on. Both citizens and the government (which exists only by the "consent of the governed") are enjoined to practice this discipline even when it requires great sacrifice. Thus, fidelity to a discipline of principles—rather than to notions of the social or public "good"—is the unending struggle of democracies. And the legitimacy of democratic governments and institutions depends on the quality of this struggle.

In totalitarian or feudal societies legitimacy and moral authority are, a priori, coming from God (the divine right of kings) or from ideological "truth." Fidelity is not to a discipline of principles but to the grand vision at the center of the ideology or to the king. Free societies become more like these unfree societies when they decide that some social good is so important that it justifies suspending freedom's discipline of principles.

The most tragic American example of such a "social good" is white supremacy. For centuries white Americans presumed that white supremacy was a self-evident divine right, so freedom's discipline of principles did not apply where nonwhites were concerned. But over time this lapse of democratic discipline undermined the moral authority (interchangeable here with legitimacy) of the American democracy and its institutions. The civil rights movement *disciplined* America with democratic principles, establishing the point that one's race could not mitigate one's rights as an individual. In democracies true moral authority is always man's responsibility rather than God's, and it can only be *earned* through fidelity to principle.

3

INFIDELITY

When I was eleven or twelve years old and crazy for baseball, I wanted to be the batboy for the local YMCA team. I wanted this so badly that I paid no mind to the fact that the team was all white. In the black suburb where I lived there was no organized baseball, only pickup games in scruffy vacant lots that flooded in the spring and turned to dust in July. The Y team played on a real baseball diamond with cut grass, a raked dirt infield, dugouts, and bleachers all around. The players were five or six years older than I and almost at the semipro level. They drove cars, had sideburns and girlfriends. Best of all, they played hardball and stood in there against the fastest pitching an eighteen-year-old arm could deliver. You knew it was fast because little puffs of dust would ascend from the catcher's mitt when a fastball was swung at and missed. It wasn't complicated. I had sort of dreamed my way into their world, and becoming the team batboy was the best way I knew to hold on.

My manner of application for the job was simply to hang

around. The coach avoided me for a long time, and I knew it was because I was black and that this was not an opportunity open to black kids. But I had no white competitors, so the more he avoided me, the more ubiquitous I became. I was at the age when wanting something very badly involves as much denial as longing. I knew about segregation and knew, on some level, that I was heading into a brick wall. But between the flowering of my dream and that brick wall, denying what I knew only too well allowed me to enjoy the sweetness of aspiration itself.

Things turned my way one day when I picked up a couple stray bats and handed them to the coach. I had done a hundred little jobs like this to make myself the solution to his stoop-labor problem, but on this day I finally saw a look of resignation in his eyes. He shook his head as if to wonder at his own helplessness, and then he began to give me orders. The orders meant I was hired, and I was exhilarated. I learned every player's bat, and at home games I quickly mastered the batboy's art of speed and unobtrusiveness. I could retrieve the newly dropped bat after a play, get it back into the dugout bat rack under the right name, and get the next man on deck his bat in one unbroken circle of movement. After games and practices I pounded the dust out of the bases, packed them in the coach's trunk, bucketed loose balls, bagged the catcher's equipment, and last, made sure the field and dugouts were completely denuded of team equipment. For all this I received absolutely nothing, though I hoped for a team cap that would finally force my snickering friends to see that I really was team batboy.

This was not to be. On the Saturday morning of our first away game I arrived at the Y early to load up the bus we were taking to a famous semipro ball field in South Chicago. The players were excited and playful when they arrived, and I looked forward to this first bus ride with the team.

It was when I was pushing the last few bags into the bus's hold that I noticed that the entire bus had gone silent. When I looked up, I saw eyes in every window, and they were all trained on me. I knew instantly that I had come to the brick wall that had been waiting for me all along. What an effort it had taken not to acknowledge it, as if all by myself I was going to will evil out of the world. But here it was finally, almost welcome for the relief it brought.

Still, there had been a great momentum in this entire effort to become a batboy, and that momentum—a kind of good faith—would not let me stop just because reality was finally showing itself. So I stood aside as the bus driver locked the hold, and then I walked straight to the bus's door. But the coach was already descending the boarding steps as I got there. He paused for a second to meet me with his eyes, and then he stepped down to the sidewalk and put a huge hand on my shoulder.

"I'm sorry," he said. "But they don't allow coloreds in the park we're going to. And that's the way it's going to be for all the away games. I can't use you anymore."

The same momentum that had led me to offer myself up in this way made me start to resist, to say something, to beg or protest or both. But then it was as though my very insides dropped out and I was utterly hollow. No words ever came. He patted my shoulder, then climbed back into the bus. I wanted to cry, felt all the precursors for a collapse into tears, but I did not cry, and I never cried. Encircled by all those eyes, I turned around and walked back into the YMCA. I will never forget the sanctuary of the huge revolving door at the front of the Y, nor the words that I said to myself as I passed through it: "This really happened, didn't it. And it's really bad."

Segregation was, of course, an institutionalized infidelity to democratic principles. But to say this is only to state a fact. Incidents like this gave this fact an emotional history. Through them the societal infidelity marked the human being—and here it marked the coach and all the players as well as myself. Back then I would have denied *any* mark. Who is tougher than a twelve-year-old boy? And even today I am certain that racist rejections like this do not cause low self-esteem in their victims. They cause disenchantment with the world. My self-esteem was not diminished in the least by what happened to me on that Saturday morning. That is not how injustice is absorbed. That morning I had had what I would much later understand to be an existential experience. This had been an encounter with the absurd, and the world was simply no longer as firm for me as it had been. So my loss of faith was not in myself; it was in the world. Ironically, this put me a little above the world and gave my own judgments a new authority. I did not become a Nietzschean superman, free to define the world on my own terms. But a new voice, and a new will, opened within me. If anything, this experience was a passage to higher self-esteem.

Ten years later, in early June of 1968, I was sitting with my parents in a hotel room in Cedar Rapids, Iowa, watching my mother across the room silently crying. I was to graduate from college that weekend, and my parents had driven up from Chicago for the ceremony. While they slept that first night—and while I embarked on a weekend-long graduation party—Robert Kennedy was shot and killed in the Ambassador Hotel in Los Angeles. Greeted with this news at breakfast, my parents—especially my mother—were as shattered as I had ever seen them by a public event. My mother was a strong, even commanding, woman, and I had seen her cry no more than a few times in my entire life.

And probably what happened next was triggered precisely by the fact that tears were so uncharacteristic of her. But the mere sight of her sitting by the hotel window, eyes wet over the assassination of Robert Kennedy, sent me into a paroxysm of rage. She had said quite clearly what saddened her. And it had nothing to do with any silly feeling for the Kennedy mystique. She had never particularly liked or trusted any of the Kennedys. She was sad, she said, because Bobby Kennedy's assassination, coming on the heels of Martin Luther King's assassination, meant that history had lost a chance. She kept repeating that history had lost a chance. But the idea that racial overcoming had come to depend on the presidential bid of this arrogant little Kennedy sent me over the top. I had by then come into a new, uncompromising idea of what it meant to be black. Blackness had suddenly become that year—well before even King's assassination—more and more defined as a will to power, as an imperative by masters rather than a plea by slaves. So it was slavish to think that black advancement was somehow dependent on the good offices of a white man without half the gravitas of black leaders like King or James Farmer or Malcolm X. Thus, for twenty minutes I berated the newly assassinated candidate with more fury than I might have mustered for George Wallace, who—it was vogue to say—was at least an honest bigot.

The fact is that we live different lives than our parents, no matter how much we love them and they us. We have a separate experience to contend with. My parents were classic civil rights people. I had grown up watching them struggle against an unapologetically racist America. In their generation protest had to be persuasion, since they were vastly outnumbered in a society that took white supremacy as self-evident truth. Like most people in the King-era civil rights movement, they were Gandhians because nonviolent passive resistance was the best way to highlight white racism as an immorality. Their rejection of violence, even as a weapon against racial oppression, gave them the extraordinary power of moral witness—the great power of the early civil rights movement. What could America think of itself when passive freedom riders were beaten or when a little black girl in crinoline and pigtails—an image of perfectly conventional human aspiration—had to be escorted into school past a screaming white mob?

This kind of moral witness transformed America forever, and its very success meant that it had, in fact, *persuaded* America. But what do all the postures of Gandhian passive resistance look like when the enemy has been persuaded? Suddenly the nonviolence that looked courageous in the face of the mob looks a little obeisant and supplicating when the mob disappears, when the government itself passes laws ending the segregated way of life the mob stood for. My parents believed with all their hearts in the moral power of turning the other cheek, but by

1968 this strategy was passé and Dr. King himself was a bit of an anachronism.

My generation had a new and different mandate. Our job was not to persuade; it was to replace passivism with militancy.

A few weeks before my parents arrived for graduation, I had led the black students on my campus into our college president's office unannounced with our generation's favorite instrument of confrontation: a list of demands. As I read these demands to the president, with all the militant authority I could muster, I allowed the ashes from my lit cigarette to fall in little gray cylinders onto the president's plush carpet. This was the effrontery, the insolence, that was expected in our new commitment to militancy. But it had not been preplanned.

I had unthinkingly lit a cigarette—a Kool, the black brand of the day—just as our march reached the administration building. As we wound our way through the building up to the president's office, I had looked for ashtrays—the bourgeois in me insisting on propriety—but found none. And as the leader of this march, I could hardly wander off to find one. So I kept moving up the stairs, right past the president's startled secretary, and into the inner sanctum of his office, lit cigarette in hand.

And once face-to-face with the president—thirty or so black students crowding into the office behind me—I had an epiphany: I should not worry about putting the cigarette out. It was exactly the gesture I was looking for. Its stinking, roiling smoke and its detritus of ash made the point that we were a new black generation operating under a new historical mandate. No more long-suffering, "go-limp" passivism. The bourgeois Martin

Luther King would never deign to smoke at such a moment, if at all, which was exactly why I had to. Our point was that black power would no longer come from being better than whites; it would come from *not* being better.

My parents heard about all this from other parents when they arrived. They broached the subject with me in a tone of grave disappointment. My cigarette had given away the high ground, they said, and invalidated the protest. It was all Kingism, the civil rights credo, the beauty and power of passivism. They spoke as if my entire youth had not been an instruction in the manipulation of moral power.

It was the next morning that I went to their room hoping to say something reasonable about the position my generation was in. But the sight of my mother crying over Bobby Kennedy brought an end to reason, and suddenly I was filled with the same militancy and outrage that had prompted the cigarette ploy in the president's office. And at the heart of this anger was an empowering feeling of license—the feeling that being black released me from the usual obligation to common decency and decorum. I was perfectly justified in spilling cigarette ashes on a beautiful carpet and in disdaining Bobby Kennedy. I was licensed to live in a spirit of disregard toward my own country.

Where did this kind of black anger come from?

Conventional wisdom, as well as black protest writing, suggests that it comes from the wound of oppression and that it is essentially an outrage against injustice. My humiliating rejection at the hands of the YMCA baseball coach, even for the lowly position of batboy, would perfectly illustrate the conventional understanding of how people are psychically wounded and made

angry by oppression. The theory is that each such wound fires
more and more anger and alienation in the soul of the oppressed
until there is an inevitable explosion. In Richard Wright's protest
novels, *Native Son* and *The Outsider,* there is a clear determinism
between the wounds inflicted by a racist society and the deadly
outbursts of violence in which his black protagonists murder
whites. Against the backdrop of wounding oppression, murder
is shown to be a futile and pathetic attempt to control one's fate
and, thereby, to reclaim one's humanity.

But, in fact, I did not work myself up for either of these displays
of "black anger" with memories of my racial mortifications. My
batboy debacle, and all the other indignities and deprivations of
a segregated childhood, never crossed my mind as I prepared to
confront my college president. There is no determinism between
one's racial wounds and the acting out of black rage—a phrase
that came into use only *after* the 1964 Civil Rights Bill. Oppression,
in itself, pushes people neither to anger nor to revolution. If it
did, black slaves would have been so relentlessly rebellious that
slavery would have been unsustainable as an institution. It is
wishful thinking in those who rightly abhor oppression to see
it as a kind of dialectic that leads automatically to the rages that
eventually topple it. Slavery might never have ended had not
larger America—at the price of a civil war—decided to end it.
The slave's rage meant nothing and brought only the lash.

Anger is acted out by the oppressed only when real weakness
is perceived in the oppressor. So anger is never automatic or even
inevitable for the oppressed; it is *chosen* when weakness in the
oppressor means it will be effective in winning freedom or justice
or spoils of some kind. Anger in the oppressed is a response to

perceived opportunity, not to injustice. And expressions of anger escalate not with more injustice but with *less* injustice.

Wounds and injustices create only the potential for anger, but weakness in the oppressor calls out anger *even when there is no wound or injustice*. In both the best and the worst sense of the word, black rage is always a kind of opportunism.

On the way home from my batboy humiliation, I knew only that all protest would be futile. Racism was not *racism* to me then. It was not an outrage but an impersonal and immutable feature of the world, like snow in winter or rain in spring. I was not going to be a batboy, and anger was not relevant to me, because there was no ambivalence about this in the larger society for anger to work on. I never even bothered to tell my civil rights–obsessed parents, because they would only have brought me more humiliation by protesting something that simply wasn't going to change. I was quite calm by the time I got home, certainly not happy but not especially sad either. By midmorning I was on to other things.

But ten years later I was nurturing anger as the central feature of my racial identity. I was bringing imagination and even a certain work ethic to the expression of black anger. What had changed in those ten years? The broad answer is that America had moved out of its long age of white racism and into a new age of white guilt. A moral ambivalence and guilt around race had opened in white America that could be worked on by black anger. By 1968 black anger and militancy had replaced the passivism of the King era as the best means to opportunity and power for blacks.

4

A CERTAIN KNOWLEDGE

If the president of my college, Dr. Joseph McCabe, was rattled when this gang of black students burst into his office, there was no sign of it as he came smiling from behind his desk to greet us. This was well before the era of the pained and solicitous college president, and his smile was meant only to suggest a certain largesse and command. He would handle us like any other intrusion on his business day, unflappably, and with grace and dispatch.

I began to read the list of demands as he moved back behind his desk and sat down. I read slowly, looking for a tone and rhythm of just suppressed anger. He had seen my cigarette by this time, and as I got to about the fourth demand, I could see that it was all becoming too much for him. This was the age of housemothers, jacket-and-tie Sunday dinners, and professors who lopped off a full letter grade for each grammatical error. There was no precedent for this sort of assault on authority, no administrative manual on how to handle it. I saw something like real anger come over his face, and he grabbed the arms of his chair as if to spring himself up. Here, finally, was the assertion of authority I had expected. I girded myself, determined to give back as good as I got.

But his arms never delivered him from his seat. I will never know what thought held him back. I remember only that his look turned suddenly inward as if he were remembering something profound, something that made it impossible for him to rise up. Then it was clear that the cigarette would be overlooked, and that he would not seriously challenge us in any way. In that instant we witnessed his transformation from a figure of implacable authority to a negotiator empathetic with the cause of those who challenged him—from a traditional to a modern college president.

He said that he knew there was something to our protest and that the college, too, wanted to make things better. For appearances' sake, he said he wasn't entirely happy with the term "nonnegotiable demand"; still, he promised to give serious consideration to each demand. And he did. To my great regret today, many of those unfortunate demands were later implemented in one form or another. On that day we ended on an almost collegial note with handshakes all around and promises to quickly follow through. By then my cigarette had burned down to the filter and simply gone out. On the way out I slipped the dead butt into my pocket.

I know two things about Dr. McCabe that help explain his transformation before our eyes into a modern college president: he was a man of considerable integrity, and he did not deny or minimize the injustice of racism. He had personally contributed money to Martin Luther King's Southern Christian Leadership Conference when this was not typical of college presidents. Thus, on some level—and in a way that may have caught him by surprise—he would have known that behind our outrageous behavior was a far greater American outrage.

And in this intransigent piece of knowledge was the very essence of what I have called white guilt. Dr. McCabe simply came to a place where his own knowledge of American racism— knowledge his personal integrity prevented him from denying— opened a vacuum of moral authority within him. He was not suddenly stricken with pangs of guilt over American racism. He simply found himself without the moral authority to reprimand us for our disruptive behavior. He knew that we had a point, that our behavior was in some way connected to centuries of indisputable injustice. So he was trumped by his *knowledge* of this, not by his remorse over it, though he may have felt such remorse. Our outrage at racism simply had far greater moral authority than his outrage over our breach of decorum. And had he actually risen to challenge us, I was prepared to say that we would worry about our behavior when he and the college started worrying about the racism we encountered everywhere, including on his campus.

And this is when I first really saw white guilt in action. Now I know it to be something very specific: the *vacuum of moral authority* that comes from simply *knowing* that one's race is associated with racism. Whites (and American institutions) must acknowledge historical racism to show themselves redeemed of it, but once they acknowledge it, they lose moral authority over everything having to do with race, equality, social justice, poverty, and so on. They step into a void of vulnerability. The authority they lose transfers to the "victims" of historical racism and becomes their great power in society. This is why white guilt is quite literally the same thing as black power.

5

WHITE GUILT

It was thirty years later, in 1998, when I pulled into San Luis Obispo for a bite to eat and noted that I had no need to find a black person. This was a college town, and I wondered what a black student would do if I swerved in to the curb, hopped out of the car, and shouted, "Say, chief. Is there a house where I can spend the night?" Today you meet another black and neither of you has much specialized racial knowledge to share. Segregation generated that sort of knowledge, and without segregation you can get good information from almost anyone. Maybe the self-segregation of blacks on college campuses and in some workplaces at least partly involves a longing for that old racial bond—the chance to concretely help and be helped by each other. But bonds that came automatically under oppression now require a self-consciously politicized racial identity that insists on a bond when there is no concrete need for one.

Paradoxically, the black identity today involves a degree of nostalgia for some of the certainties that were the unintended consequences of racial oppression—the security of an enforced group identity and group unity, the fellow feeling of a shared fate, the comfort of an imposed brotherhood and sisterhood, the idea of an atavistic, God-given group destiny. But freedom has disrupted all this. As fervently as black America always longed for freedom—envisioning it as God's promised land—the actual experience of freedom has involved a sense of loss. Today there is much talk of "community" among blacks just as America has ceased to impose community on us. And in this talk there is a looking backward for that lost Eden when segregation made racial interdependence our only option. Today it is fashionable among blacks to say that integration was a failure, which is to imply that our true strength is in separatism. Today you can witness blacks everywhere enforcing on themselves the very separatism and community that segregation so recently imposed—black churches, civil rights confabs that are far more social than political, "state of black America" gatherings as if we still share a singular destiny, black professional associations by the hundreds, black student associations of every variety, even a congressional black caucus, not to mention black caucuses in many state legislatures. Now in the promised land of freedom we reach for the lost Eden of separatism. If we can just get together, squeeze ourselves into some sort of "unity," we can overcome. But racial unity is politically self-defeating in freedom, since it leaves the nicely unified race to be taken for granted by power. Freedom can be seized only by individuals. And the fact is that we blacks *are* free.

It was of course white guilt that *enforced* greater freedom for blacks. In the thirty years since I had seen it so clearly on Dr.

McCabe's face, white guilt had generated a new social morality in America that made racial prejudice utterly illegitimate. And it would take a powerful phenomenon like white guilt—as opposed to simple goodwill—to accomplish so difficult a task.

Because white guilt is a vacuum of moral authority, it makes the moral authority of whites and the legitimacy of American institutions *contingent* on proving a negative: that they are not racist. The great power of white guilt comes from the fact that it functions by stigma, like racism itself. Whites and American institutions are stigmatized as racist until they prove otherwise. Stigma is behind the now clichéd white disclaimer: "Some of my best friends are . . . ," which is a way of saying, "I might be white, but I am not a racist, because I have friends who are black." Whites know on some level that they are stigmatized by their skin color alone, that the black people they meet may suspect them of being racist simply because they are white. And American institutions, from political parties and corporations to art museums and private schools, not only declare their devotion to diversity but also use racial preferences to increase the visibility of minorities so as to refute the racist stigma. Surely genuine goodwill may also be a part of such efforts. But the larger reality is that white guilt leaves no room for moral choice; it does not depend on the goodwill or the genuine decency of people. It depends on their fear of stigmatization, their fear of being called a racist. Thus, white guilt is nothing less than a social imperative that all whites, from far-left socialists to Republican presidents, are accountable to.

So I was able to walk through downtown San Luis Obispo without fear of racial insult because white guilt has given America a new social morality in which white racism is seen as disgraceful.

Moreover, this social morality is not a dissident point of view urged on society by reformers; it is the establishment morality in America. It defines propriety in American life so that even those who harbor racist views must conform to a code of decency that defines those views as shameful.

And this social morality—born of white guilt—became the establishment morality because it answered the problem of white guilt. It brought moral authority and legitimacy to a society that had acknowledged its history of racism. The American democracy simply could not move forward after the civil rights era without adding to its great democratic principles an explicit *social morality* based on the insight that racism is immoral. An achievement of the civil rights movement was to make the point that multiracial democracies require a moral consciousness that rejects race—and, for that matter, gender, ethnicity, class, and sexual orientation—as a barrier to individual rights. So this social morality was meant to be the finishing touch for the American democracy, a concept of the social good that would make democracy truly democratic and, thus, legitimate.

Back in the pre–civil rights era—the age of racism—racial bigotry itself was part of the moral establishment, an element of propriety. Back then the baseball coach who rejected me was only reinforcing a social order that saw racism as essential to common decency. Blacks, of themselves, constituted an indecency in many public places. And this coach was only carrying out the civic duty of "avoiding trouble" by barring me from traveling with the team. So, again, one has to be grateful to white guilt for bringing about possibly the greatest social transformation in American history.

content of your chrach

6

THE NEW CONSCIOUSNESS

Going north on Highway 101, out of San Luis Obispo just past Paso Robles, you pass through one of those stretches of the West where the landscape seems to exist as a frame for vastness itself. You see a rim of low mountains to the east that slope down westward to a rather desolate plain of dry riverbeds, scrub growth, and the occasional dinosaur-necked oil rig—all making a great space that turns the driver inward. And until I pass into the powerful KGO radio signal from San Francisco, I am even without the Clinton row on the radio. Still, only a month after the wagging finger, it is hard not to have tangential Clinton thoughts even in this void. What comes to mind is how important the word "consciousness" was back in the sixties.

Behind the moral evolution that allowed President Clinton to survive what would surely have destroyed President Eisenhower, there was also an evolution of "consciousness." In the sixties this was almost a wastebasket term with many meanings and themes: racial and gender liberation, Eastern spirituality, baby-boomer grandiosity, the Dionysianism of "sex, drugs, and rock 'n' roll," antiwar and antiestablishment sentiment, revolutionary politics, and then the loose popularizations of Marx and Freud through which most of all this was filtered. But the unity of these themes—what made them all elements of a single consciousness—was their common challenge to traditional American authority in virtually all its forms.

By the mid-sixties—after America's acknowledgment of racial hypocrisy and the beginning of the age of white guilt—"consciousness" began to function like adolescent rebellion, as an almost petulant alienation from traditional authority that set off a rebellious search for new authority and identity. The so-called counterculture, born of this consciousness, reflected both this crisis in traditional authority and the search for new sources of authority. Vietnam and the emergence of feminism only further radicalized this process, so that by the late sixties "consciousness" began in a faith that something was deeply and intractably wrong at the core of American life.

In the vastness between Paso Robles and King City, where the world is both profoundly present and profoundly absent, it seems clear that this "consciousness" is what transformed President Clinton's sin from something immutable into something relative. It seems to be making marital infidelity, so condemned by traditional authority, into something rather slight relative to the infidelity that leads to racial inequality. And it seems to make traditional authority itself look the spinster—alarmed over sex but indifferent to oppression.

This "consciousness" has transformed the moral character of America. Where did it come from?

* * *

I remember first hearing the admonition to "raise your consciousness" at a black power rally in the summer of 1967. The rally was held at night in a small church on the South Side of Chicago, and despite the sweltering August heat, the overflow crowd was restless. People lined the walls and clogged the front door in blatant violation of fire codes, yet there were no policemen to be seen. This was the era of race riots, and the mere sight of a policeman's uniform would have seemed a provocation. The crowd was especially large because word had gotten around that the comedian Dick Gregory would be speaking. Already famous as a comedian, Gregory had recently gained new fame within the black community for openly expressing his racial militancy despite his very lucrative nightclub career. Such was the magic of the new mania for blackness that it could inspire selflessness in a man with much to lose. And that night it was Gregory who made a mantra of the phrase "raise your consciousness." *woke*

I knew the phrase had a Marxist derivation, but Gregory made it correspond to a much-valued attitude—if not a philosophical stance—in black life: hipness. This attitude comes out of the experience of oppression in which survival requires one to have a *separate knowledge* from that of the oppressor. The world lies constantly to those it oppresses, and to survive oppression one must not only be "hip" to those lies but also nurture a deeper awareness of the world as it really is. This more existential and subversive awareness of the "real" world is hipness. And the hipster is a kind of existential hero who preserves his humanity (amidst his oppression) by seeing through to the irony and absurdity of his situation. The true hipster is never surprised—is therefore "cool"—because he already knows. That night Dick Gregory was the quintessential hipster offering up the Marxian idea of social determinism as an existential fact of the "real" world that we blacks would have to "be hip to" if we wanted power.

He never actually called it social determinism, but that is what it was. And he used it as a "hip" truth to show us how profound our victimization as blacks actually was. Like others in the new group of "militant" black leaders that was emerging at the time, he used the hipster's knowing posture to "school" us, to suggest that we had deluded ourselves into thinking that our victimization was a slight thing. Here he put himself in respectful opposition to Martin Luther King. For King, and the older civil rights generation, racism was simply a barrier, a tragic aberration in an America that was otherwise essentially open and fair. But Gregory demanded that we "raise our consciousness," that we "get hip" and understand that racism was not a mere barrier but the all-determining reality in which we lived.

That night was my first encounter with the essentially Marxist vision of American racism that would frame the racial debate for the next three decades. It was a precursor to the now common argument that racism is "systemic," "structural," and "institutional." Of course, this was not formal Marxism (Gregory never used the word); rather, it was a loose conceptual borrowing from Marxism. The point was that ugly human prejudices like racism did not just remain isolated in the hearts of racists. These dark passions worked by an "invisible hand" to generate societal structures that *impersonally* oppressed. As people simply conformed to mundane standards of social decency, they executed bigotry and shaped society around it without necessarily feeling animus toward minorities. When I met discrimination as a child, the perpetrators often apologized for upholding a custom they did *not* believe in. Many seemed perplexed by what they were doing. They could tell me that they hated racism even as they executed its strictures, and *I* was often invited to feel sorry for *them*.

The Marxian emphasis on structures and substructures gave the new militant leaders of the time an infinitely larger racism to work with, a systemic and sociological racism that was far more "determinative" than the simpler immoral racism of the Martin Luther King era. If whites moved to the suburbs for a better life, black leaders now had a concept of racism large enough to see the diminished inner-city tax base as a systemic injustice to blacks. If blacks were disproportionately drafted to fight in Vietnam because they were disproportionately poor and out of school, then this too could now come under the umbrella of racism.

Of course, social determinism had long been a common idea among black intellectuals. Richard Wright's great 1940 novel, *Native Son,* had made the social determinism of race a feature of literary naturalism. But only in the mid-sixties, *after* the strongest antidiscrimination laws in history had been passed, did a new generation of black leaders begin to argue that racism was a determinism as well as a barrier—and thus a far greater enemy of black freedom than had previously been imagined. Logic would have argued the other way, that the new civil rights legislation meant that blacks were facing a far less deterministic racism. And surely black leaders would have agreed with this logic if they were responding to actual racial oppression. But they weren't. They were responding to white guilt.

Dick Gregory was just the first black leader I encountered in the then brand-new age of white guilt. Martin Luther King had delivered his great speeches in the age of racism to a resistant America still minimizing the human toll of its racism. For King's generation of leaders racism was a barrier in the path to black freedom, and the goal was to remove it. But for this new generation of black leaders, racism existed within a context of white guilt, within a society that suffered a vacuum of moral authority precisely because of its indulgence in racism. Thus, America and all its institutions suddenly needed something from blacks—a people who in the past had been needed for little more than manual labor. By the mid-sixties white guilt was eliciting an entirely new kind of black leadership, not selfless men like King who appealed to the nation's moral character but smaller men, bargainers, bluffers, and haranguers—not moralists but specialists in moral indignation—who could set up a trade with white guilt.

The most striking irony of the age of white guilt is that racism suddenly became *valuable* to the people who had suffered it. Racism, in the age of racism, had only brought every variety of inhuman treatment, which is why the King generation felt that extinguishing it would bring equality. But in the age of white guilt, racism was also *evidence* of white wrongdoing and, therefore, evidence of white obligation to blacks. King had argued that whites were obligated to morality and democratic principles. But white guilt meant they were obligated to black *people* because they needed the moral authority only black people could bestow. Only the people themselves—meaning of course the black leadership— could vet the white moral redemption, the white deliverance from racism. Thus, white guilt made racism into a valuable currency for black Americans—a currency that enmeshed whites (and especially American institutions) in obligation *not to principles* but to black people as a class. (Notice that affirmative action explicitly violates many of the same principles—equal protection under the law, meritorious advancement—that the King-era civil rights movement fought for.) Lacking other sources of capital, blacks embraced racism as power itself.

What was new for me on that hot August night was that Dick Gregory was not fighting to end racism as King had always done; he was giving us the ideas we needed to enlarge it. I didn't understand at the time that it was precisely the fact that King had won America's acknowledgment of racism's evil that, in turn, made racism so valuable to blacks. This acknowledgment was simultaneously an acknowledgment of obligation to racism's victims: blacks. Gregory was redefining racism from a barrier to a determinism in order to expand the territory of white obligation. White guilt had inadvertently opened up racism as the single greatest *opportunity* available to blacks from the mid-sixties on—this for a people with no other ready source of capital with which to launch itself into greater freedom.

A fact that has escaped notice in the decades since the civil rights victories is that, after those victories, racism became a bifurcated phenomenon in America, so that we have been left with two kinds of racism. The first is the garden-variety racial bigotry that America has, sadly, always known—the source of racial oppression and discrimination. But the new and second kind of racism is what might be called *globalized* racism. This is racism inflated into a deterministic, structural, and systemic power. Global racism seeks to make every racist event the tip of an iceberg so that redress will be to the measure of the iceberg rather than to the measure of its tip. It is a reconceptualization of racism designed to capture the fruit of the new and vast need in white America for moral authority in racial matters. True or not, global racism can have no political viability without white guilt. What makes it viable is not its truth but the profound moral need that emerged in mid-sixties white America.

In the age of racism there was very little global racism because there was very little white guilt to appeal to. Also, actual racism was so self-evident that civil rights leaders did not need to put forth inflated estimations. With a simple lunch-counter sit-in they could elicit the most vivid displays of brutal white racism for the TV cameras—ketchup poured on the hair of black students, cigarettes ground out on their backs. But after America entered the age of white guilt in the mid-sixties, racism began to go underground and even diminish. Just as white guilt began to make white racism into an opportunity for blacks—an occasion for "demands"—it became harder to provoke the racist theater that the South had so willingly offered up for early civil rights leaders. For black leaders in the age of white guilt the problem was how to seize all they could get from white guilt *without* having to show actual events of racism. Global racism was the answer. With it, the smallest racial incident proved the "global truth" of systemic racism.

This is why one black man being beaten by police in Los Angeles could trigger a massive riot in which some sixty people were killed. By the terms of global racism one racist incident proved the rule of systemic racism. And the rioters themselves, having absorbed global racism as a theme of racial identity, launched a riot to the scale of systemic racism rather than to the scale of the single racist event—assuming that Rodney King's beating was in fact motivated by racism. The ominous billows of black smoke rising above Los Angeles—large and thick enough to dim the sun—were also meant to suggest the scale of white obligation. The rioters said, in effect, that the rage which set this city on fire was against a systemic racism that went far beyond the police assault on one man. Systemic racism would have to be answered with systemic redress. Here they served well the national black leadership and affirmative action beneficiaries everywhere. Black students across the country who had never suffered discrimination, much less been beaten by white policemen, would continue to enjoy the systemic redress of affirmative action with a new sense of entitlement.

People said these rioters were crazy because they burned up their own neighborhoods and killed far more of their own people than the police ever did. But, in fact, they were working a rather sophisticated adaptation to white guilt. Ingeniously, they globalized what was very likely a necessary police beating into an agonized national debate on the state of black America—a debate that invariably expands both white obligation and black entitlement. Certainly they did great injury to their community, but, by their lights, they also reinforced black leverage against white guilt.

It was social determinism that made global racism possible. Determinism was the *idea* that moved racism from the level of discriminatory events to the level of "impersonal" and "structural" forces that worked by "invisible hand" to stifle black aspiration even when real racists were nowhere to be seen. When racism is defined as a determinism, then whites and American institutions are part of a cultural pattern ("white privilege") that *automatically* oppresses blacks; and blacks are *automatically* victims of this same pattern. As the Los Angeles rioters instinctively knew, global racism enables blacks to frame racism to the scale of white guilt rather than to the scale of white racism—too weak these days to count for much.

But the ground had been prepared for the nineties riot by the famous sixties riots (the Watts riot of '65, the Detroit and Newark riots of '67, and many others), which established a virtual riot paradigm in which the scale of violence was always far out of proportion to the triggering event, usually a real or rumored instance of polite brutality. Interestingly, these truly devastating riots occurred just at the dawn of the age of white guilt, and not before. They occurred at the precise historical moment when it was clear that white America would see them as authentic expressions of black rage and would respond to them with understanding rather than disregard and withering suppression. And for this newly receptive white audience they were always a lesson in scale. The disproportion between an isolated racist incident and days of chaotic violence that took lives and destroyed vast stretches of property was meant to suggest the disproportion between mere racist events and the much broader structural determinism that kept blacks down. The scale of violence was the true scale of racism, and these sixties riots taught white America—by illustrating this proportion—the scale of its obligation to blacks. Systemic racism would have to be answered with systemic redress.

What proves that black rioting in the sixties and the nineties has been more a manipulation of white guilt than an honest expression of black rage is that whites themselves have only rarely been the targets of violence. There were no raids into white neighborhoods, no guerrilla warfare against institutions and businesses, no terrorist acts against public works. The damage was always to fellow blacks and within black neighborhoods. No doubt individual rioters felt rageful, but the targets of their rage belie their true goal: to persuade rather than hurt their oppressor, to turn white paternalism from hostility to generosity, and to establish a global racism that would bring global redress.

When I visit university campuses today, black students often tell me that racism is everywhere around them, that the university is a racist institution. When I ask for specific examples of racist events or acts of discrimination, I invariably get nothing at all or references to some small slight that requires the most labored interpretation to be seen as racist. Global racism allows these students to feel aggrieved by racism even as they live on campuses notorious for almost totalitarian regimes of political correctness—and to feel more aggrieved than black students did forty years ago, *before* the civil rights victories. This is because their feeling of racial aggrievement is calibrated to the degree of white guilt on university campuses and not to actual racism. When I ask if they feel racially aggrieved away from campus at their summer jobs, they often look surprised, as if the question is not relevant. But then most say they don't see as much racism at their summer jobs. Global racism prevails precisely where whites and institutions most aggressively search for moral authority around race. Even announcements of a new commitment to "diversity" within an institution will very likely *increase* feelings of racial aggrievement in minorities. We blacks always experience white guilt as an incentive, almost a command, to somehow exhibit racial woundedness and animus.

* * *

And global racism has given the age of white guilt another of its familiar features: the "race card," or blackmail by white guilt. Threatened with a stigmatization that can gravely injure businesses and ruin careers, whites can be pressured into treating the merest accusation of racism as virtual proof of global racism. When an executive at Texaco Corporation was overheard making a remark that some thought racist, no one in the company hierarchy had the moral authority to combat the prima facie impression of racism. In flight from stigmatization, Texaco paid $750 million to the corrupt diversity industry even though the "racist" executive was found to have only repeated a nonracist term he picked up at a company-sponsored diversity-training program. Texaco, Coca-Cola, and Toyota are only a few of the corporations that have paid hundreds of millions of dollars to avoid "global" stigmatization as racist.

The race card works by the mechanism of global racism: even a hint of racism proves the rule of systemic racism. So these corporations never pay to the measure of any actual racism; they pay to the measure of racism's hyped-up and bloated reputation in the age of white guilt.

In the O. J. Simpson murder trial, defense attorney Johnnie Cochran used the fact that Detective Mark Fuhrman lied on the witness stand about having ever used the N word to assert that the entire mountain of evidence pointing to Simpson's guilt was likely contaminated with racism. Here again was the disproportion that global racism always seeks. From a man who lied to conceal an embarrassment, Fuhrman was transformed into someone who could very likely be a craven racist, a person capable of malice aforethought who might prowl Simpson's property planting evidence against him everywhere. So powerful was global racism in the case that even the possibility that this implausible caricature might be true was given more weight than solid DNA evidence linking Simpson to the murders. The mere suggestion of racism proved the rule of virulent racism. What this meant in this court was that the bar for "reasonable doubt" was completely defined by global racism. And the court itself— like most American institutions in this age of white guilt—was so bereft of moral authority in racial matters that it could not restore proportionality to the proceedings. It could not stop the Fuhrman caricature from carrying the day. Racism was allowed to become a kind of contaminating ether that wafted through and dispelled even the hardest evidence.

Johnnie Cochran succeeded in making the trial a contest between the empirical evidence and global racism, between fact and the *reputation* of racism for distorting and manipulating fact. What he gambled on was that the court—on television before the world—would have to show itself, above all else, *deferential* to racism's distorting power. Though this black lawyer saw racism everywhere, he did not gamble his case on the court's being racist; he gambled it on the court's being obsessed with showing its utter freedom from racial bias, its determination to let even a hint of racism disqualify sound evidence. Johnnie Cochran instinctively understood that the court—an American institution in the age of white guilt—was infinitely more concerned with its own moral authority and legitimacy than with the truth. He knew the court would allow global racism to be the standard for "reasonable doubt" not because it was a reasonable standard but because it gave the court—in this trial of a famous black man—much-needed legitimacy where race was concerned. In sum, he knew that the court would essentially forgo the evidence against Simpson simply to prove that it was not biased against Simpson.

Of course, Cochran could not have invented global racism just for use in this trial. It had to have existed already in American culture, and it had to have a self-evident plausibility and power that he could pit against the plausibility of empirical fact. In the age of racism, racism itself had been such a power. White supremacy had been a higher and more sacred law than the law of the courtroom, so that whites who murdered blacks rarely even went to trial or, if they did, walked free no matter the evidence against them.

In 1955 the conviction of the white murderers of Emmet Till (the black teenager famously murdered for looking at a white woman in Mississippi) would have fractured the social order of the segregated South, so the facts in the case meant nothing and the murderers walked. White supremacy had to be served, just as white guilt was served in the Simpson case. Both Till's killers and Simpson enjoyed a "race card." Both invoked their race to gain immunity from the law. (Interestingly, in today's age of white guilt, there is even talk of reopening the Till case.)

Does the historical symmetry of all this amount to historical justice—Simpson's black race card evening the score with the Till killers' white race card? I don't think so. It only makes the point that we have not yet achieved an America in which race cannot suspend the law.

7

RACE AS DESTINY

Dick Gregory had been preparing the ground for the Simpson trial on that long-ago, hot August night on the South Side of Chicago. Simpson, I believe, would never have gone free in 1967. Neither white guilt nor the concept of global racism that blossomed to exploit it was fully developed at that time. White guilt was just beginning back then as a naive exhilaration over all that might be done by the Great Society. America still thought it could roll up its sleeves and plunge into its redemption with the same pragmatic zeal that had lifted the country out of depression, won world wars, and rebuilt Europe and Japan—redemption by good ol' American can-doism.

But race was not a war to fight or a depressed economy to overcome. It was a tangled ugliness of the human heart and a very complex symbiosis between two kinds of Americans and two American experiences. More simply, it was—as set against the principles of democracy and the Judeo-Christian ethos—a portal to evil, but an evil that was seemingly as hardwired into the human psyche as the simple human need for hierarchy, for the idea of a God-intended pecking order of colors.

In 1967 America had only just acknowledged actual racism. There would have been no idea of global racism to rescue an O. J. Simpson. It fell to people like Dick Gregory and the new generation of militant black leaders to up the ante on white guilt by "hipping" us to the concept of racism as a determinism, as opposed to racism as a mere event. It fell to them, in other words, to invoke a new black *consciousness*. Our centuries-long symbiotic relationship to white America had evolved, yet again, this time with the advent of white guilt. And our group consciousness needed a strategic update. How to be black in a world of white guilt? Where did strategic advantage lie? And on that hot night on the South Side—and on countless later occasions—my consciousness was, in fact, raised to meet the new *opportunity* that was white guilt.

I learned to remake the world around the central truth of global racism. To do this I took on the notion—as hipness itself—that man, loosely speaking, was a cipher, a non-individuated creature, who was pushed and abutted by forces much larger than himself. I did not altogether deny free will, and certainly continued to exercise it in my life, but intellectually I took on the sophistication that it was largely a delusion of the common man, a kitschy individualism that Americans liked to flatter themselves with. (One of the delights of Marxian-tinged ideas for the young is the unearned sense of superiority they grant.) Change would not come from selfish individualism and a "fascistic" faith in free will (the roots of inequality); it would come from overthrowing the structural forces that oppressed. Then you had to put good structures in the place of bad ones—the sort that ushered people toward equality.

And I learned that my group identity as a black was more important than my individuality. After all, I hadn't been made to live in segregation because of who I was as an individual. And no amount of individuality would slip me past the structural barriers of segregation that held all people of my color back. White racism had made my race the limit of my individuality. But now the new black consciousness I was learning from people like Gregory wanted me to voluntarily, even proudly, do the same thing that racism had done: make my race more important than my individuality. Unwittingly, this new consciousness came into perfect agreement with the first precept of white racism. This meant that Dick Gregory and George Wallace ("segregation forever") were saying the same thing: that race was destiny—the same axiomatic American truth that the civil rights movement had just won a great victory against. So now, as I was coming into greater individual freedom than I had ever known, the new militant black consciousness wanted me to embrace again my race as my destiny. In the age of racism I had wanted freedom as an individual; in the age of white guilt I was learning to want power as a black.

To up the ante on white guilt this new black consciousness led blacks into a great mistake: to talk ourselves out of the individual freedom we had just won for no purpose whatsoever except to trigger white obligation.

8

RESPONSIBILITY IN THE AGE OF RACISM

I was twenty-one years old when I heard Dick Gregory speak that night. I had come straight from my summer job as a Chicago Transit Authority (CTA) bus driver to hear him. Working as a lowly substitute for vacationing regular drivers, I had spent a long hot summer driving up and down the main drags of Chicago's South Side, usually from the late-afternoon to the early-morning hours. It was a very naked encounter with the human condition, and I saw and learned a lot. But the swing-shift hours were killing, and I had gone that night to hear Dick Gregory a little depressed at the thought of three more weeks of hard driving and jagged sleep before deliverance came in the form of my senior year in college.

It had never entered my mind not to finish those three weeks. This was the best-paying summer job I'd ever had and, after spending the three previous summers in the Chicago stockyards, it was a relatively clean job as well. Moreover, I had been raised around what might be called the "good man" ethic. A good man was the one you turned to when work got really tough, when quality counted, when deadlines had to be met. A good man always finished what he started. Such men were quiet figures of dignity in my working-class neighborhood. And in the name of this ethic I had continuously held some sort of job since my sixth-grade paper route. I had bought my own clothes since the seventh grade, and paid the main portion of my college tuition when the time came.

It was a neighborhood friend—scrounging, as we all were, for a summer job open to blacks—who put me onto the CTA job. Both of us were so surprised and grateful to be hired that we brought a special intensity to our training. We would be "good men." So we were quick studies when it came to the complex coordination of wielding a loaded city bus through rush-hour traffic while punching transfers, making change, keeping time, and negotiating the random personalities that appear at urban bus stops. Sad to say, but our sense of possibility was still conditioned by segregation, and in the back of our minds was the idea that bus driving might have to be more than a summer job. For my friend this turned out to be true.

But beneath our gratitude was one of those ugly psychic tensions generated by segregation. In slavery blacks were not free, but they were also not entirely responsible for their lives. Slavery was a form of incarceration that dehumanized its victims as much by denying them responsibility for their lives—by providing them with a subsistence existence—as by denying them freedom. Freedom is crucial to a decent life, but only in being responsible for one's life can one take *agency* over it. And agency—the sovereignty and will that we have over our individual lives—is what makes us fully human. To its credit, segregation gave us agency over our lives by allowing us to be fully responsible for ourselves. But it also cruelly denied us the freedom to use our agency for much more than subsistence. So segregation was yet another dose of the absurd: you can have responsibility but not much possibility; you can have sovereignty over your life but not enough freedom for it to matter much.

My father, who was born in the South in 1900, had plenty of responsibility, but he was pushed out of school in the third grade to work in the fields. When I was growing up he worked as a truck driver, but he could not join the Teamsters union, which in turn meant he could not receive a union wage—or union protection on the job. The union in fact wanted his job for its white members. So his race meant that he lived in an insecure nether land with no harbor among either capitalists or socialists. It meant, for example, that he had to hide his home ownership—managed on a subunion wage—from his employer for fear that he would be fired for "getting above himself." It meant also that he had to dodge the union even as he begged it for membership. He lived like a citizen in a totalitarian society—the agent of his own life yet living within an absurd circumstance where his very humanity, not to mention his aspirations, was deemed subversive to the state.

Yet he restored three ramshackle homes to neat lower-middle-class acceptability by collecting bricks, discarded lumber, cast-off roofing shingles, and chipped porcelain bathtubs and sinks, and then by working and working—as if work were a kind of alchemy—until he had a rentable property. And there were other dreams—a "bug juice" extermination business, a garage-building enterprise, a trade in house paint—all workable, if limited, possibilities that he spotted within the cracks of a rigidly segregated society. Yet he could not buy property where his sweat might become real equity, or do business where real profits were possible and where banks didn't run the other way. His society quite literally labored to defeat his ambition even as it left him entirely responsible for his life and family. When my parents died, the houses they had labored so hard to develop had been all but engulfed by ghetto blight. The family signed them over to their nonpaying renters for nothing, happy to be rid of the liability.

RESPONSIBILITY AS A TOOL OF OPPRESSION

Let's call this situation a crucible—or an absurd bind that forever denies one the opportunities to meet adequately the burden of responsibility one must carry, and that suppresses one's higher aspirations almost altogether. It was the psychic tension of this crucible that made my friend and me so grateful for our bus-driving jobs. In this crucible blacks were literally oppressed and punished *with* responsibility. Common human responsibilities—getting an education, owning a home, raising a family—were very often touched by futility, defeat, and pathos. Segregation tried to take all the reward and possibility out of responsibility so that all that remained was its weight of worry and its burden of struggle. Thus, a heavy and often futile responsibility was the primary *experience* of racial oppression. If many whites, too, struggled in poverty under heavier burdens of responsibility than they could bear, there was still more freedom and possibility open to them. For blacks, this Sisyphean struggle with responsibility was the condition of oppression itself into which all the other indignities—discrimination, intimidation, humiliation—were absorbed.

In high school—as if serving an apprenticeship in segregation's crucible—I was turned down for a lowly stock boy's job at JCPenney, for a fast-food job at one of the first McDonald's, for paper routes in white neighborhoods, for caddying jobs on golf courses, for busboy work in restaurants, for any work that was either clean or reasonably well paid. I saw my white peers step into and out of these same jobs as whim and the need for pocket money dictated. Because this kind of segregation made it so much harder for me to meet my responsibilities, it also made it easy for me to confuse responsibility itself with racial injustice, to *experience* them as one and the same. When I was in the fields picking tomatoes and onions on the truck farms just south of Chicago rather than caddying at Olympia Fields golf course, the *experience* of being responsible was in fact an experience of injustice. And it was no doubt all the emotions generated by life inside this sort of crucible—some acknowledged, some not— that must have set me up for what happened in that hot church as Dick Gregory spoke. At the time it felt like an epiphany, a sudden new knowledge. But it wasn't a new knowledge at all. It was something that I had always known, only then it exploded numinously to life.

Somewhere toward the middle of Gregory's long riff I was overcome by a feeling of utter relief. It was as if some old and grinding worry—one I had considered permanent, as inevitable as nature—had simply passed away. I felt exhilarated, wildly happy—this despite the fact that Gregory was clearly pulling for the era's all-purpose emotion: black anger.

But there was another meaning within his words. He was also saying that a racist society had inflicted responsibility on us while denying us the freedom to do much with it. In other words, he was describing the crucible in which responsibility was a tool of oppression. And his clear implication was that responsibility was therefore *illegitimate* where blacks were concerned. Responsibility made fools of us. Worse, it made us complicit in our own oppression. As we labored away with the odds fixed against us, we only reinforced the racist social order that oppressed us. Ever the sneering, smiling hipster, he created a rube character for our derision—the "good Negro." Here was the honest, hardworking black man laboring to make a decent life for himself and his family, and by doing so reinforcing segregation as a perfectly commendable social order. Gregory was talking about men like my father, and this bothered me. But he softened his point by universalizing it. We were all honorable fools; all "good Negroes" unwittingly bolstering the forces that kept us down. Here we could all laugh at ourselves. We were suffering inside a crucible not because we were bad or lazy but because we were *responsible*. Responsibility was our tether to oppression.

But why did all this fill me with such relief? Why did it make me feel happy?

Though I could not have said it at the time, this was the moment—listening to Gregory go on about "good Negroes"—when I realized that the civil rights movement had truly won. Dick Gregory and all the other new militant leaders were really just being redundant. America had already agreed with them.

Two years before this night President Johnson had launched the Great Society in his famous Howard University speech by saying: "You do not take a person who, for years, has been hobbled by chains and liberate him, bring him up to the starting line in a race and then say 'You are free to compete with all the others.'"

Here the president of United States had virtually described the crucible blacks had endured, saying for all the world that blacks had been "hobbled" by that old oppressive formula—full responsibility with little freedom—so they had never been allowed to become competitive. Johnson clearly realized that full responsibility had been an unfair and oppressive burden on blacks. His Great Society was, among other things, a *redistribution* plan for responsibility by which he asked white America to assume considerable responsibility for black advancement. Thus, by implication, the president of the United States had agreed with the new militants that it was morally wrong—given what blacks had been through—to ask them to be fully responsible for pulling themselves up.

So suddenly in American life the matter of responsibility was qualified by a new social morality. If you were black, and thus a victim of racial oppression, this new morality of social justice meant you could not be expected to carry the same responsibilities as others. The point was that the American society no longer had the moral authority to enforce a single standard of responsibility for everyone because—by its own admission—it had not treated everyone the same.

It is true that Muhammad Ali lost his heavyweight boxing crown when he refused the military draft—a universal responsibility for American males at the time—but it is also true that he only added to his legend by doing so. When he said, "I ain't got no quarrel with the Viet Cong," even his enemies understood his point. Where was the moral authority to ask this black man, raised in segregation, to fulfill his responsibility to the draft by fighting in a war against a poor Asian country?

Standing there in that church I realized that no one—least of all the government—had the *moral* authority to tell me to be responsible for much of anything. And this realization, blooming in the mind of a twenty-one-year-old after a hard day's work, was like winning my own private revolution. I could hardly stand still.

And the moral authority that America suddenly lacked passed into me as pure moral power. *Suddenly I could use America's fully acknowledged history of racism just as whites had always used their race—as a racial authority and privilege that excused me from certain responsibilities, moral constraints, and even the law.*

Up to this point I, like my father before me, had lived like a citizen in a totalitarian state. But what happens when an authority that was totalitarian—against which you had no recourse—admits that it was wrong, that it violated and dehumanized you? For one thing, you lose a degree of fear. I knew, of course, that America was going to continue holding blacks accountable to its basic laws. But I also felt a new fearlessness in showing my disdain for whatever the country might hold me accountable to. Not only was this totalitarian power broken, but now I was the one—as a victim—who possessed an almost reckless moral authority. Now I could shame and silence whites at will. With this moral authority there was the power to better defend myself against racism, but there was also a new, abusive power very similar to the abusive power that had been wielded against me—a power of racial privilege deriving solely from the color of my skin. This power to shame, silence, and muscle concessions from the larger society on the basis of past victimization became the new "black power." Then, as this power supported the next generation of civil rights leaders, it evolved into what we call today "the race card." But back on that hot August night I only felt a weight drop from my shoulders as I began to understand that my country was now repentant before me. I now possessed a separate power that it could only appeal to, appease, or placate. Now America had to prove itself to me.

I have already discussed the narcotic effect of all this. This was the inflation that, months later, would lead me to spill cigarette ashes on Dr. McCabe's fine carpet. But far more important, this great infusion of moral authority gave blacks the power to imprint the national consciousness with a profound new edict, an unwritten law more enforceable than many actual laws: that no black problem—whether high crime rates, poor academic performance, or high illegitimacy rates—could be defined as largely a black responsibility, because it was an injustice to make victims responsible for their own problems. To do so would be to "blame the victim," thereby repeating his victimization. Thus, in the national consciousness after the sixties, individual responsibility became synonymous with injustice when applied to blacks.

When America acknowledged its racism, it effectively made blacks into the nation's official and, seemingly, permanent victims—citizen-victims, as it were, for whom demands of responsibility are verboten lest the larger nation seem to be oppressing them all over again. If President Johnson's Howard University speech meticulously spelled out white America's responsibility for black uplift, there was not a single reference to black responsibility. Even though the president was about to spend billions of dollars on blacks, he still lacked the moral authority to spell out the ways blacks needed to be responsible for their own advancement. It was a classic white-guilt speech, implying that racial inequities are overcome solely by the efforts of whites and American institutions. (Today's college presidents routinely make such speeches when they stand to proclaim their institution's commitment to "diversity.") The speech insistently and conspicuously refused to imagine blacks outside a framework of victimization. And no president since Johnson has done any better.

President Roosevelt's New Deal had frankly asked for sacrifice and hard work from the average American because it was clear that whatever the government did had to be met by the responsibility of the citizens. But Roosevelt was seeking prosperity, not redemption. It is nothing less than stunning that in the four decades of racial reform since the sixties, and amid constant racial debate, there has not been a single articulation by an American president of how blacks might so much as even share responsibility for their own advancement.

THE REDISTRIBUTION OF RESPONSIBILITY

But I couldn't have known any of this as I stood listening to Dick Gregory. I just felt greatly relieved that the burden of responsibility I had always known was suddenly without moral authority. I remember thinking a little nervously of my father. Would he buy Gregory's implication that responsibility was a "trick bag" for blacks, a submission to white authority that extended our oppression? I could not imagine it. Responsibility was his great faith; he would never see the logic in thinking of it as something that "blamed the victim."

But this thought gave me only brief pause. I was convinced that we were in a new era of civil rights. Even whites as high as the president now agreed that responsibility had been oppression itself for blacks. So here, I thought—with the arrogance my generation was famous for—was a case of age having no advantage over youth. My father had no more experience of this new era than I had.

And if, in the long run, time proved me wrong, in the short run it proved me right. By the night of my encounter with Dick Gregory the goal of the civil rights movement had escalated from a simple demand for equal rights to a demand for the redistribution of responsibility for black advancement from black to white America, from the "victims" to the "guilty." This marked a profound—and I believe tragic—turning point in the long struggle of black Americans for a better life.

Black America faced two options. We could seize on the great freedom we had just won in the civil rights victories and advance through education, skill development, and entrepreneurialism combined with an unbending assault on any continuing discrimination; or we could go after these things indirectly by pressuring the society that had wronged us into taking the lion's share of responsibility in resurrecting us. The new black militancy that exploded everywhere in the late sixties—and that came to define the strategy for black advancement for the next four decades—grew out of black America's complete embrace of the latter option.

Racial militancy and anger are, of course, easy emotions to feel when your country finally admits to having oppressed you for no reason other than the color of your skin. But if blacks had left America in the mid-sixties for a land of their own where no whites dwelled, this militancy and anger would have been beside the point. Without whites it would have had no object, no point. And instead of the interminable preoccupation with race and social justice that we blacks developed after our civil rights victories, there would have been only the hard work of making the group competitive with other groups and societies.

But we did not leave America in the sixties. We remained inside the same society that had wronged us, a society that suddenly needed to show great concern for us on pain of its own moral authority. Why not look to this society to take responsibility for what it had done to us? America had been responsible for our suffering, why not for our uplift?

Black militancy, then, was not inevitable in the late sixties. It came into existence *solely* to exploit white guilt as a pressure on white America to take more responsibility for black advancement. Effectively, black militancy and white guilt are two sides of the same coin. Neither exists but that the other exists. Together and separately their goal is always to redistribute responsibility for black uplift from blacks themselves to American institutions. So black militancy, for all its bluster of black pride and its rhetoric of self-determination, is a mask worn always and only for the benefit of whites.

Authentic black militancy, of the sort that Malcolm X at times seemed capable of, always embraced responsibility as power itself. It demanded only the freedom and equal treatment under the law that would allow responsibility to be the same fount of hope, power, and advancement in blacks that it was for others. If Malcolm X railed ferociously against white America, he never called for a redistribution of responsibility for black uplift to whites or American institutions. His was a self-help black militancy that was naturally skeptical about what others would actually do for blacks. You might call it "hard-work" militancy, since it was built around the difficult principles of self-sacrifice, delayed gratification, family unity, individual initiative, entrepreneurialism, and so on. If it carried an ugly theme of separatism, it more importantly focused on racial redemption through human development and nation building. What made this militancy authentic was that it truly sought to restore an oppressed people to human dignity through real development and without an enmeshment with or dependency on the guilt of whites.

But the black militancy that actually emerged in the sixties— what might be called "white-guilt" militancy—was the opposite of this. Because it was really a strategy to redistribute responsibility to American institutions, it literally argued that blacks could not be fully responsible for their own advancement—this simply to make the point that whites had to be more responsible for it. Thus, since the sixties, black leaders have made one overriding argument: that blacks cannot achieve equality without white America taking primary responsibility for it. Black militancy became, in fact, a militant belief in white power and a correspondingly militant denial of black power.

Black leader after black leader argued that we could not pick ourselves up by our own bootstraps, because we "don't have any bootstraps." But this humiliating plea for white intervention only projected whites as powerful and blacks as helpless. So, finally, we embraced a black militancy that argued nothing more strongly than our own perpetual weakness—or, put another way, our inferiority. To be a proud and militant black after the sixties, you screamed black power in order to induce the application of white power. And you lived by an ethic that still sees full responsibility as oppression, if not racism, when applied to blacks. Still today, the best way to make a black leader mad is to say to him that black Americans are capable of being fully responsible for their own advancement.

This is a black militancy of inferiority that assumes the *continuing* inferiority of the people it tries to speak for. And this is where it again meshes so perfectly with white guilt, which always assumes a nearly intractable black inferiority. Because American institutions stand in such pressing need of moral authority, they cannot wait for blacks to develop a true equality of competence out of which they could win entrée on merit. Therefore, since President Johnson's Howard University speech, racial reform has focused on what Johnson called equality "as a result."

The corruption of "results"-oriented racial reform is that it separates racial reform from all accountability to the actual development of excellence and merit in black Americans. The inferiority imposed on blacks by four centuries of oppression is ignored as institutions shoehorn minorities into their midst (by lowering standards) simply to get the "result" that shows the institution to be beyond racism. Preferential affirmative action, the classic "results"-oriented racial reform, tells minorities quite explicitly that they will not have to compete on the same standards as whites precisely so they can be included in American institutions *without* in fact achieving the same level of excellence as whites. The true concern of "results" reform is the moral authority of the institution. Minority development is sacrificed to the magnanimity of the institution.

Neither black militancy nor white guilt has ever been at all accountable for overcoming—or even moderating—the terrible underdevelopment that oppression imposed on blacks. But the "results" reform that these two forces generate *does* redistribute responsibility for black advancement to American society. This redistribution has been the all-defining centerpiece of racial reform since the sixties. Moral authority comes to institutions only when they relieve minorities of responsibility (lowered standards, racial preferences). In this age of white guilt responsibility is synonymous with oppression where blacks are concerned. So whites and American institutions live by a simple formula: lessening responsibility for minorities equals moral authority; increasing it equals racism. This is the formula that locks many whites into publicly supporting affirmative action even as they privately dislike it.

It is also the formula that keeps black America underdeveloped even as we enjoy new freedom and a proliferation of opportunity. No worse fate could befall a group emerging from oppression than to find itself gripped by a militancy that sees justice in making others responsible for its advancement. Of course white guilt—this voracious vacuum of authority—more than wants the responsibility that black militancy is determined to give it. It needs and demands it. But this sad symbiosis overlooks an important feature of human nature: human beings, individually or collectively, cannot transform or uplift themselves without taking *full* responsibility for doing so. This is a law of nature. Once full responsibility is accepted, others can assist as long as it is understood that they cannot be responsible. But no group in human history has been lifted into excellence or competitiveness by another group. No group has even benefited from the assistance of others without already having taken complete responsibility itself—complete to the point of saying that we appreciate your desire to help, but the help itself is unwelcome for the weakness it breeds. This is precisely the leap of faith that transforms people from slaves into their own masters.

All this was especially ironic, since we had just won the great battle for our civil rights by taking mastery over our own fate. Others joined our struggle, but clearly we did not allow the movement to be contingent on what others did. We also have never allowed our performance in sports, music, literature, or entertainment to be contingent on whether or not others helped us.

These last points are important because they illustrate a pattern. Wherever and whenever there is white guilt, a terrible illusion prevails: that social justice is not a condition but an agent. In this illusion social justice procures an entirely better life for people apart from their own efforts. Therefore it makes sense for minorities to make social justice a priority over their individual pursuit of education and wealth. (There will always be time for development when social justice is won, goes one rationalization. Another argues that a lack of social justice still stymies individual ambition despite the fact that blacks now live in freedom and are surrounded by opportunity.) The reason for this illusion is that white guilt *wants no obligation to minority development.* It needs only the *display* of social justice to win moral authority. It gets no credit when blacks independently develop themselves. So white liberals and American institutions (along with a corrupt black leadership) keep seducing blacks with social justice as though it were also *developmental.* When universities bring in black students with SAT scores 300 points below the student average, the illusion is that by arranging this diverse "result" they will magically develop black students until this 300-point gap disappears. But, of course, there is no evidence that this gap ever disappears or even shrinks. Nevertheless, institutions win their moral authority around race. This is why white guilt generates only "results," affirmative action–style reform—reform that brings moral authority to whites without the bother and expense of minority development. And to achieve this corruption white guilt commits another one: it constantly portrays problems of minority underdevelopment as problems of injustice.

Since the sixties, black educational weakness has been treated primarily as a problem of racial injustice rather than as a problem of blacks rejecting or avoiding *full* responsibility for raising their performance levels. Thus we got remedies pitched at injustices rather than at black academic excellence—school busing, black role models as teachers, black history courses, "diverse" reading lists, "Ebonics," multiculturalism, culturally "inclusive" classes, standardized tests corrected for racial bias, and so on. All this but no demand for parental responsibility, for harder work on reading, writing, and arithmetic.

When there is no white guilt vying for responsibility over minority struggles, there is no incentive to distort these problems into instances of injustice. We blacks, then, remain entirely responsible for them whether or not we get help from others. In music, literature, sports, and entertainment our deficiencies are, thus, simply deficiencies that we overcome in the way all people overcome deficiencies: through skill development, innovation, and relentless practice.

People wrongly dismiss black achievement in these areas for reasons that can be ascribed only to racism—that our compelling excellence follows from a mere genetic advantage. The fact is that we are good at sports and music because we subject ourselves to unforgiving standards of excellence and then work ferociously to meet those standards. Ruthlessly, we allow absolutely no excuses. The same poverty and deprivation that afflict us as we walk to school in the morning afflict us later in the same day on the playground or in the tenement basement where we practice obsessively on a cheap electric keyboard. The difference is that white guilt makes no appearance on that playground or in that basement. There is no carnivorous white need standing between us and the pursuit of excellence. No pity. Thus, excellence is allowed to entice us with its own intrinsic joys and rewards; and we come in thrall to it. Suppose Marvin Gaye or Duke Ellington or Richard Wright or Kareem Abdul-Jabbar or Condoleezza Rice or millions of others (all people from humble beginnings born in the age of open racism) had let their pursuit of excellence be somehow contingent on the ministrations of white guilt, on the spiritually withering interventions of needy, morally selfish white people betting on the cliché of black inferiority rather than on the natural *human* longing for excellence that resides in us all?

Black achievement in music and sports should never be dismissed; rather, it should point the way to black achievement in all other areas. Here is the self-possession, the assumption of full responsibility, the refusal to trade on one's plight, the engagement with the broader American mainstream, the insistence on excellence as the currency of advancement—all of which makes blacks utterly irrepressible in these areas. And then, in concert with this, come the hard work, imagination, discipline, sacrifice, relentless effort, and—most important—*openness* to competition with *all* others that gave us our Ellingtons, Ellisons, and Kings.

* * *

If a young black boy cannot dribble well when he comes out to play basketball, no one will cast his problem as an injustice. No one will worry about his single-parent home, the legacy of slavery that still touches his life, or the inherent racial bias in a game invented by a white man. His deficiency will be allowed to be what it is—poor dribbling. And he will be told to "tighten his game," which simply means to practice more. Very likely his peers will taunt him mercilessly, and even adults will give him no hugs to assuage his self-esteem. Very likely he will live through all this without the consultations of a father. Moreover, the standard of excellence for dribbling will be so high that many will not reach it and nothing less than virtuosity will satisfy it. When and if he meets this standard, he will be told "You bad" even by his competitors. This expression, of course, means its literal opposite: that he has at last earned entrée into a fraternity of nothing other than excellence. Surely he will feel proud of himself as a result.

But if this boy's problem is reading or writing rather than basketball, white guilt will certainly prevent even a modified version of this natural human process from occurring. Career-hungry academics will appear in his little world, and they will argue that his weaknesses reflect the circuitous workings of racism. His reading and writing problems will be seen to follow from countless racial and psychological determinisms that make it impossible to ask that he and his family be fully responsible for overcoming these problems.

The boy will not be asked to truly work harder, nor will he be guided in the mastery of sentence structure, parts of speech, and verb tenses. No one will righteously insist that he speak correctly

They are still enslaved like a fat person toresh... to resh himself

(as certain people once did for me). Yet he will be an object of abstract compassion for everyone. And permeating his classroom, like a stalled weather pattern, will be a foggy academic relativism in which scholastic excellence is associated with elitism, and rote skill development with repression. Yet just beyond the window of his classroom, on the pockmarked basketball court with the netless and bent hoop, another weather pattern prevails. On that court almost nothing is forgiven, and he will be "blamed" and held entirely responsible for all his deficiencies. And all through the torpor of a day structured to spare his feelings around reading, writing, and arithmetic, he will long to be on the other side of that window, where *everything* is asked of him.

The greatest black problem in America today is freedom. All underdeveloped, formerly oppressed groups first experience new freedom as a shock and a humiliation because freedom shows them their underdevelopment and their inability to compete as equals. Freedom seems to confirm all the ugly stereotypes about the group—especially the charge of inferiority—and yet the group no longer has the excuse of oppression. Without oppression—and it must be acknowledged that blacks are no longer oppressed in America—the group itself becomes automatically responsible for its inferiority and non-competitiveness. So freedom not only comes as a humiliation but also as an overwhelming burden of responsibility. Thus, inevitably, there is a retreat from freedom. No group that has been oppressed to the point of inferiority is going to face the realities of new freedom without flinching. Almost always,

HIGHLIGHT

oppressed groups enter freedom by denying that they are in fact free, this as a way of avoiding the daunting level of responsibility that freedom imposes.

Freedom becomes a great problem for an emerging group because of all the illusions the group falls prey to as it buffers itself from the humiliations and burdens of freedom. Instead of taking *full* responsibility for our underdevelopment, we convince ourselves that we should pursue social justice and that this will agent us into a competitive equality with whites. We avoid the terrifying level of responsibility that freedom imposes by arguing that *whites* should be responsible for our development. We even define full black responsibility as an intolerable injustice. Our understandable fear of freedom has led us to bank our fate on an absurdity: that we can develop by taking *less* responsibility for ourselves. We have defined freedom as a kind of heaven in which the inhabitants are forgiven responsibility. Thus, we have conspired to throw away the greatest power we have: *complete* responsibility for our own development, an opportunity that we finally have the freedom to assume.

How could a people that has survived centuries of slavery and segregation—through ingenuity, imagination, and great courage—get this confused, this alienated from man's most elemental power: responsibility? Because freedom scared the hell out of us—our first true fall, our first true loss of innocence— and because there was nothing less than a locomotive of white guilt coming our way and hungering to prop us up in our every illusion. White guilt has wanted nothing more than to confuse our relationship to responsibility, to have us feel responsibility as an injustice, a continuation of our oppression. It exploited

our terror of freedom in precisely the same way that plantation owners once exploited our labor. Whites needed responsibility for our problems in order to gain their own moral authority and legitimacy. So they set about—once again—to exploit us, to encourage and even nurture our illusions, to steal responsibility from us, to take advantage of our backwardness just as slave traders had once done on the west coast of Africa. Suddenly, in the age of white guilt, we were gold again.

BRO: And so, once again severed from responsibility and in service to white need, we became—as if by some cruel karmic principle—slaves again, our fate the responsibility of others. Always in slavery and segregation our genius went into the pathetic task of adapting to the needs of a master, of fashioning a face for survival under his power. And so it is that the terrors of freedom have only deepened our slave mentality, our belief in the mask that manipulates the master. For us, group pride does not come from our capacity to stand our ground and compete equally with all others; it still, tragically, comes from our genius for shape-shifting, for working over the master for the rube that he is.

Still imprisoned

Property is the other side of this coin.

like a kid who threatens to run away

11

QUITTING

When Dick Gregory finally ended his monologue, the crowd was exhilarated, a little manic. It was nearly midnight, but as we spilled out into the muggy night there was a morninglike energy, as if we had skipped past the night and run straight into the new day. My friend and I should have gone straight home to grab a few hours of sleep before work the next day, but there was too much to talk about. Sleep was unthinkable. So in my '54 Chevy, with its slipping clutch and leaking oil, we drove to the Robin's Nest on Stony Island and talked frenetically over the jazz until closing time. Then, near Sixty-third Street, we found a blues club that took us almost to dawn. By the time we turned onto the Dan Ryan Expressway southward toward home, the sun was up and the new day was already hot.

After only a few miles I pulled off the expressway and found a phone booth. Without giving myself time to think, I called the dispatcher at the Seventy-fifth Street bus barn and quit the best job I had ever had. I was scared and my voice was a little weak, but I did the deed. I quit. I walked back to the car with a proud if nervous smile, and admonished myself—against a sudden "bourgeois" anxiety over what my father would say—to stay strong. I knew it was an irresponsible and even futile gesture, since the job was scheduled to end in three weeks anyway. Still, it meant something to me, and I was glad I had done it.

Since well before this night I had been struggling within myself to undo the strict civil rights conditioning of my youth, especially the Gandhian propriety of humility and nonviolence by which a demeanor of quiet dignity highlighted the outrages of segregation. This conditioning required an *acceptance* of American moral authority, a faith that America was good and great in every way except for its racism. Thus, we blacks—like Martin Luther King—should *conform* to every code of common American decency so that our dress, speech, and graces shamed the racist notion of our inferiority. This is not to say that the dignity so many blacks displayed in that era was only an act. It was not. Still, there was an unspoken admonition that we must behave better than whites—show ourselves more morally civilized—in the hope that they would find their guilt and end segregation.

But if all this dignity was not an act, it was also not self-referential. It was aimed, as an instrument of social revolution, at whites. And this is what—after America's great acknowledgment of racial wrongdoing—made it so intolerable to me. In the age of white guilt, long-suffering dignity in blacks was an Uncle Tomish redundancy. White guilt had triggered a racial role reversal. Suddenly whites had to prove their broader humanity by displaying a human dignity that was above racism. And blacks, now validated as fully human by America's acknowledgment of racism, were all but commanded to show the indignation and outrage of full human beings—thus the new militancy, the rageful new black consciousness.

The point is that we blacks organize our political identity— our consciousness of ourselves as blacks—around those themes that most effectively manipulate white America. And the stoic "Rosa Parks" black identity of the civil rights era had actually worked. This was the identity that morally "manipulated" white America into an open acknowledgment of its racism and, thus, ushered in the age of white guilt. Dick Gregory was simply a part of my personal white-guilt reeducation program. He, along with the new generation of militant leaders, was schooling blacks in the best identity for this new age. Ideas like social determinism and the rejection of responsibility by blacks inspired precisely the angry and petulant black identity that best coerced white guilt.

This leadership did not want to rely on ideas, ideologies, or careful historical analyses. It wanted blacks to act reflexively out of identity itself. So militance toward whites became a litmus test of "blackness." Even if you felt no such militance, you developed a militant posture simply to secure your black identity. This was an ingenious use of *identity as power* because it enabled these leaders to base their power on something deeper and more reliable than ideas. The litmus test for *being black* required one to accept racial victimization not as an occasional event in one's life but as an ongoing identity. When victimization is identity, then the victim's passionate anger can be called out even when there is no actual victimization. In other words, the victim's anger can be relied on as a political force. The remarkable achievement of the sixties black militants was to create a substantial political power for themselves out of the identity of their people. This identity, of course, was not power in itself. White guilt was the power, and this identity was the leverage militant leaders used to access that power.

Unfortunately, all this gave blacks a political identity with no real purpose beyond the manipulation of white guilt. Worse, because this identity was thought to be absolutely essential to black power, it quickly became the most totalitarian and repressive identity that black America has ever known. All dissent became heresy, punishable by excommunication, because anything less than uniform militancy weakened the group's effectiveness with white guilt. Dick Gregory was not just spelling out this new identity; he was also making it clear that our identity—our "blackness"—was contingent on our militance. And failing the litmus test of militancy incurred the Uncle Tom stigma.

I quit my bus-driving job in order to *be black*. My friend understood this and promised to quit in short order himself. Actually he did not quit for over a year and even put off college to continue making the first good money of his life. But on that hot morning we both sincerely believed he would quit within days. In any case, he was my only witness, the only one who, as we said back then, had had his "consciousness raised" along with mine. He understood what I was doing. On the drive back home we constituted a little black avant-garde driving down the Dan Ryan Expressway. We were ahead of our friends, who would at first sneer at our report of the night, but then be impressed and ready for similar nights of their own. Within months every black I knew of my own generation—except for a few bourgeois and a few Pentecostals—was a militant. And they all came to militancy in the same way that I did, by what might be called a gesture of identification.

When identity is everything because group power derives from it, a mere command of ideas or ideologies is not enough to identify. There must be an actual, if only symbolic, gesture of some kind that expresses militant disregard for the American "system." A good gesture of identity will show contempt for the "white world" and a corresponding reverence for "blackness"— this is a vaguely spiritual vision of racial redemption through a "blackness" that reverses white racism by projecting black supremacy and white moral inferiority. Quitting my job was a rejection of white authority and personal responsibility in a society where racism made a joke of such responsibility in blacks. This gesture was clearly silly, but at the time it did exactly what a gesture of identification should do: it made me feel that I had a better world to belong to than the racist world I had always lived in, a counterworld that stood in contrast to the corruption of white America. But I had to *do* something to make common cause with that world. So I quit.

Of course, I knew I would continue to have business with America, and three weeks later I was in fact using my chauffeur's license to drive a bus again, this time a school bus back in my college town. But there was something different about this new job. I felt buttressed by my black identity. This identity was suddenly the source of a wonderful new *self-esteem* that was utterly independent of white America. I felt that simply "being black" aligned me with one of the world's great stories of long-suffering innocence, and that this redounded to me as moral superiority over white Americans and, thus, gave me an immunity from their *judgments*.

All my life I had had ingrained in me the expectations, rules, and values of broader America, but suddenly all this conditioning was suspect. Didn't it represent the internalization of oppression itself? Wasn't the desire to dutifully educate myself little more than complicity with a racist status quo? "Blackness"—automatically and instantly—gave me the self-esteem I would have to work a lifetime for in white America. So I didn't care so much about advancing in American life. Back in college that fall my grades plunged, and though this would have mortified me earlier, now it didn't bother me in the least. I cared nothing for what my professors thought of me, or for what affect all this would have on my prospects for graduate school. With my new esteem I could suddenly *bear failure* in the "white" world that would have been unthinkable before. I didn't know it at the time, but it was my first experience of how group identity can take the place of accomplishment as a source of *individual* esteem.

Quitting my bus-driving job had been a gesture of identification with black *authority*—a morally superior authority in this new age of white guilt that was not offended by the self-destructiveness of quitting a perfectly decent job when there was still college to pay for. Blackness gave me a new esteem that was in no way contingent on performance or success in the white world. In fact, if I failed it would only be an opportunity to better display black victimization in the court of white guilt. So, for the price of a gesture of identification, I got enough esteem to be a little above the world I actually lived in. Like Black Panthers strapped in ammunition belts and storming the California legislature, or

Stokely Carmichael in a dashiki screaming "black power," I could enjoy a superiority that came to me by birthright alone.

A gesture of identification could be almost any act—quitting a job, dropping out of school, giving up Christianity for Islam, dropping one's "slave name" for a jerry-built African name, buying a weapon and learning to use it—that would show disengagement from white America and loyalty to the new black authority. Actually, the gesture of identification always required at least an element of self-destruction, a flirtation with failure in the white world, which verified black authority as the true source of one's esteem. But this was not understood in the late sixties. Then I knew only that in being black I had come into a kind of privilege.

PART TWO

AN EXPANDING GUILT

12

WHITE REBELS

At King City, Highway 101 takes an abrupt leftward turn as if to move you quickly away from something unsightly. You see a Denny's sign, a Shell or Exxon sign looming over the highway, and then you are suddenly headed due west over more ravines of rock and scrub, a bank of coastal mountains in the distance. The tiny agricultural town of King City is gone before you can adjust yourself to look for it. And when the turns finally point you northward again toward San Jose and San Francisco, you are let out on the fertile plain of the Salinas Valley—Steinbeck country, and one of California's great breadbaskets to the world. Between low mountain ranges on the east and west the earth is as flat and black as an Illinois landscape. Long, freshly planted rows are engineered for perfect drainage, sprinkled with water, and dusted with chemicals into a perfectly bankable fertility. There are no farmhouses in sight.

In this landscape, with its clear radio reception, Clinton is again ubiquitous on the car radio. At first his troubles seem especially shameful in this valley where people live so directly off the land. But, of course, this is no longer the small-town world of pernicious gossip and bluenosed fundamentalism suggested by Steinbeck's early fiction. These fields are a high-tech factory laid out on the land, and the people who own and manage them are no more likely to be scandalized by Clinton than Chicagoans or Atlantans. Baby boomers are in charge pretty much everywhere these days, and Bill Clinton is not foreign to them. He is as familiar as the sixties consciousness itself and, thus, the first president they know as a peer.

Toward the end of the age of racism, at the height of the civil rights movement, there was a moment when progressive black and white youth seemed to share an "integrationist" consciousness. White college students flooded into the South and onto the front lines of the struggle against segregation in the early sixties. The Student Nonviolent Coordinating Committee (SNCC) was as white as it was black. But in the mid-sixties, as the age of white guilt was launched by the civil rights victories, blacks began to expel whites from the cause of civil rights. This racial divergence was not only the beginning of the militant black consciousness that I fell in thrall to in the late sixties; it was also the beginning of a progressive white "youth" consciousness that was no longer centered on the struggle of black Americans.

Young whites politely accepted that blacks would have to run their own movement, and then raced to the cause of the Vietnam war. In time, many other causes—particularly feminism and environmentalism—became themes of this new youth consciousness, which ultimately became known as the "counterculture." This was the cultural and political consciousness in which Bill Clinton came of age, just as I came into black militancy in my twenty-first year.

And driving through the rich Salinas Valley, I hear this same baby boomer–counterculture consciousness on the radio, tempered very little by the decades. It is now the establishment consciousness, while traditional American values now constitute a kind of counterculture. And listening to these callers, it becomes clear to me that there is not enough raw indignation in America over Clinton's behavior to truly empower the traditionalists. For the first time since the wagging finger, it seems almost certain to me that this sex scandal will not bring down the president.

It was Vietnam that pushed the youth consciousness of the sixties far across the continuum of disaffection into possibly the worst case of generational alienation in American history—bad enough to spawn an essentially anti-American counterculture with greater moral authority than traditional America. Of course, this consciousness clearly began in civil rights because this was where America effectively confessed to profound moral corruption and hypocrisy. This was the confession—the crack in the facade of American greatness—that was then held against America as the Vietnam War escalated. Thus, it enlarged from a localized confession of racism into a broad confirmation of America's inherent evil and oppressiveness.

And then, simmering away behind all this from as far back as the fifties, was the idea that America, with its greedy "military-industrial complex," was essentially a "repressed" nation. Here a little bastardized Freud was mixed with Marx to make a rather neat formula: a sexually repressed society was necessarily a bigoted and oppressive society. Thus, the underside of postwar America's "gray flannel" conformity was social evil. But this pairing of sexual repression and social evil also had an especially appealing upside: it linked sexual openness to social virtue. The idea that a lack of sexual inhibition signified a deeper and more compassionate humanity became one of the more fabled ideas of the counterculture. Here casting aside one's sexual inhibitions was a way of opening up to one's deeper humanity and, thus, separating oneself from the dark human impulses to racism, sexism, and militarism that plagued the repressed, bourgeois world of one's parents. At the center of the sixties consciousness was always this confluence of the personal and the political where freedom from bourgeois repressions was always somehow an aspect of social responsibility. This was the counterculture consciousness that Bill Clinton encountered in the mid- to late sixties.

I believe that the most important—if seemingly incongruent—point to understand about the sixties youth consciousness is that, like the sixties black militant consciousness, it was largely a response to white guilt. This guilt is the vacuum in moral authority created by *all* of white America's moral failings and infidelities to democracy: racism, sexism, imperialism, materialism, conformity, environmental indifference, educational inequality, superficiality, greed, and so on. Thus, white guilt is a much broader phenomenon than the "race problem" from which it takes its name. Race provided the first and most conspicuous instance of infidelity to democratic principles, and the first instance where the wrong was openly acknowledged. But then the Vietnam War, escalating almost simultaneously with this acknowledgment, further injured America's moral authority in the eyes of many young people. And, in quick succession, other issues—women's rights, the plight of farm workers, degradation of the environment, black and white poverty—converged rather spectacularly to give the impression (especially to the young) that oppressiveness, greed, exploitation, and violence were the essence of the American character. The sixties were simply a time when seemingly every long-simmering conflict, every long-standing moral contradiction in American history, presented itself to be made right even as an ill-conceived war raged on. And the resulting loss of moral authority was the great vacuum that literally called the counterculture consciousness into being.

The ideas and ideologies that shaped this consciousness no doubt came from many sources—Marx, Freud, Martin Luther King, Herbert Marcuse, R. D. Laing, Chairman Mao, Lao-tzu, to name only a few. But it was white guilt—this enormous vacuum of moral authority—that called out the counterculture and the black militancy that I encountered in the sixties. Both these "counter" movements were new assertions of moral authority that hoped to combat the illegitimate authority of racist/imperialist/sexist traditional America. But if the new black consciousness wanted only the fruits of white guilt, the counterculture wanted to remake America altogether. And in many ways it succeeded.

I remember first noticing this counterculture consciousness when it seemed to enter and then take over the life of a college classmate. We had come to college in the same year but knew each other only in that small-college way in which you know all about people you don't really know. I knew that John (as I will call him) was from a well-to-do military family. He was as clean-cut as a marine and yet he dressed with just the right dash of patrician disregard. He was the first person I ever saw wear a jacket, tie, and Bass Weejun loafers with no socks to Sunday dinner—a little subversion of our midwestern dress code that spoke of an East Coast prep school background. But there was also an inescapable sense of angst about him that seemed quite real, and thus made him all the more appealing to girls. People said it had to do with a far-off father whom he seemed to both hate and admire—a figure he sometimes excoriated and at other times, rather reflexively, showed reverence toward.

This was the John we all knew, or knew about, for the first two years of college. But at the start of our junior year, John did not show up. Someone said he had gone out to California and become a hippie—a new word, as well as concept, at that time. And, as unimaginable as this seemed given the John we all knew, it was nevertheless confirmed a month later when he reappeared on a huge black motorcycle to retrieve a girlfriend before heading back to the hippie life in California. His blond girlfriend had not yet been "hippie-ized," and they made quite a sight racing around the day or two before they left—he now rather dirty-looking in jeans, fringed Indian jacket, and bandanna; she still in the tailored skirts and prim blouses of a Tri Delt, striving on the back of his powerful bike to show an excitement equal to the grand gesture they were about to make while at the same time struggling with the propriety of her skirt.

Of course, their rebellion had no connection to the social and political upheavals of the day. It was only a rather histrionic version of what psychologists call adolescent rebellion—a normal feature of human development by which the young (teen years to early adulthood) separate from parental authority to experience the world on their own. Maybe it was the far-off father—an unbending set of expectations—that pushed John to a more dramatic rebellion than most. But whatever the motivation was, it was not political. John's eyes rolled whenever a discussion veered toward politics. And without the gravity of political or social themes, it was hard to see his rebellion as anything more than an action taken to enrage an overbearing father.

What made John's rebellion seem so much grander than this was the turbulent, fast-changing world that surrounded it. In the fifties adolescent rebellion met a society that still had a strong sense of its own moral authority. Fifties rebels like James Dean and Elvis Presley were not the popular vanguard of a new dissenting politics. And Elvis only enhanced his celebrity by serving honorably in the military—thus acknowledging the moral authority of his country. But John rebelled into the age of white guilt and, thus, into a society that was growing less and less certain of its moral authority. If John's rebellion had no political motivation, if it was simply personal, it met a society where political forces and social upheaval suddenly justified—even glamorized—all kinds of rebellion. Rock stars, black militants, antiwar leaders—all their rebellions touched a broadly anti-American politics that gave them a special charisma in the sixties.

So the sixties were a time when even the most ordinary and personal acts of youthful rebellion were aggrandized by a powerful new dissenting politics that let you rebel against "the system" rather than merely your parents. In that first decade of the age of white guilt, when America's moral authority began to weaken, youthful rebellion suddenly represented a further challenge to the moral authority of American society and its institutions. Like the protests against racism and war, it seemed to represent a *historical judgment* against America. It seemed to be yet more evidence that there was something soulless and avaricious at America's core that was now coming home to roost in the rebellion of an entire generation of young—just as America's racism and militarism had come home to roost in the civil rights and antiwar movements. Thus, adolescent rebellion in the sixties, because it coincided and melded with such great transformative movements, took on a historical resonance it would never have had outside the reflected light of these movements. It came to seem like a social *movement* in its own right, a broad and happily amorphous youth movement taking on the injustice of America's soullessness.

Usually adolescent rebels are quickly humbled because they overestimate their own truth and underestimate the truth of their elders. As Mark Twain famously put it, "When I was a boy of fourteen, my father was so ignorant I could hardly stand to have the old man around. But when I got to be twenty-one, I was astonished at how much he had learned in seven years." One purpose of youthful rebellion is to put one's self at odds with adult authority not so much to defeat it as to be defeated by it. One opposes it to discover its logic and validity for one's self. And by failing to defeat it, one comes to it, and to greater maturity, through experience rather than mere received wisdom. Of course, every new generation alters the adult authority it ultimately joins. But if the young win their rebellion against the old, their rite of passage to maturity is cut short and they are falsely inflated rather than humbled. Uninitiated, they devalue history rather than find direction in it, and feel entitled to break sharply and even recklessly from the past.

The sixties generation of youth is very likely the first generation in American history to have actually won its adolescent
rebellion against its elders. One of the reasons for this, if not
the primary reason, is that this generation came of age during
the age of white guilt, which meant that its rebellion ran into an
increasingly uncertain adult authority. Baby boomers, already
rather inflated from growing up in the unparalleled prosperity of
postwar America, were inflated further by an adult authority that
often backed down in the face of their rebellion. It doesn't matter,
for example, that there was honor in America's acknowledgment
of moral wrong in the area of race. An acknowledgement of
wrong was an acknowledgment of wrong, and it brought a loss of
moral authority—and, thus, adult authority—despite the good
it achieved. And when you added to civil rights the Vietnam War,
feminism, the plight of farm workers, a new environmentalism,
a deepening animus toward materialism and corporate power,
and a "credibility gap" between young and old, you could easily
make a damning case against adult authority. No previous
generation had been served up a richer menu of social and moral
"contradictions" and "hypocrisies" with which to hammer away
at the moral authority of adult American society.

Much of this hammering may have made America a better society,
may have resolved some rather profound contradictions in American
life—the treatment of minorities and women, for example. But over
time, it also expanded the vacuum of moral authority that is white
guilt far beyond matters of race and the struggles of minorities.
This meant that issue upon issue became framed by the paradigm
of white guilt. With the environment, for example, America was

essentially cast as an oppressor—a kind of environmental "racist"—and the environment as its victim. Disregard for the environment was presumed to come from that same soullessness, imperial greed, penchant for violence, and false sense of superiority that racism came from. And, as with race, "correct" attitudes toward the environment are enforced by the blackmail of stigma, so that Americans are stigmatized with a kind of environmental racism until they prove otherwise. If you don't stand against, say, drilling for oil in Alaska, then you are displaying the soullessness and hubris thought to be endemic to the American character. You are a kind of bigot.

So white guilt may have gotten its initiating, big-bang start in race relations and America's great acknowledgment of racial wrongdoing, but it was quickly expanded by all the moral authority that America began to lose to other conflicts, especially the Vietnam War and the struggle for women's rights. Certainly the country resisted acknowledging wrongdoing in these areas, but not as confidently or for as long as it had in the racial arena, where it took centuries to break through resistance. But after racial resistance was finally breached, America forever lost a certain innocence. The country had become rather familiar with this new phenomenon of acknowledging a moral wrong. So there was certainly support for the war and even some resistance to full equality for women, but the moral landscape had already begun to change. People who took these positions were increasingly stigmatized as Neanderthals who wanted women in the kitchen, blacks in their place, and a military that opened the world for American economic exploitation. They were more and more marginalized as living incarnations of the American soullessness and greed, all that decent Americans now wanted to move beyond.

By the late sixties many in the establishment were not only acknowledging wrongdoing in race and war, but also suggesting that America suffered from a deeper, more characterological problem. All this acknowledgment—coming even from establishment figures like the grandfatherly TV anchor Walter Cronkite, who questioned the war in 1968—took moral authority away from traditional America. In the especially turbulent year of 1968, the vacuum of moral authority was so vast that some wondered if the country would stand. A conservative candidate, Richard Nixon, was narrowly elected president in that year to—among other things—stand firm against the young, many of whom were beginning to take the word "revolution" seriously. This ever-expanding vulnerability that the young sensed in America was white guilt.

And it was, in fact, *white* guilt rather than American guilt, not only because the great loss of moral authority began in white racism, but also because whites were the nonoppressed Americans, the only race/clan for which all the precepts of the American democracy fully applied, and the group that conducted the nation's affairs entirely in its own self-interest. Whites had kept blacks down, taken the country to war when it suited them, resisted pleas for equality from their own women, ruined the environment out of greed, practiced a capitalism that exploited the resources of poor countries around the world, and so on. It doesn't matter that all of this is not precisely true, or that there is another and more positive side to at least some of it, or that America—for all its transgressions—is also indisputably great. White guilt follows from a Kafkaesque *racial* stigma that all whites—even baby boomers such as my classmate John—carry like Kafka's character Joseph K., who is guilty merely because he is accused.

So while it might be true that John was essentially driven by adolescent rebellion, it was also true that his *race* was in a kind of crisis. His race—normally confident to the point of thinking of itself as universal humanity—was suddenly struggling in the first stage of its open stigmatization as racist, soulless, and greed-driven. This was the beginning of the age of white guilt, when whites in America, if not the world over, began to live a little like Joseph K., for whom accusation was the same as guilt. And worse, the Kafka allusion did not perfectly apply, because there was considerable truth to the accusation that whites were racists. Joseph K., had in fact done nothing to feel guilty over, but white Americans had been raised in a thoroughly and explicitly racist society in which racism so infused every aspect of life that it was a form of good manners—propriety itself.

Even if one had no animus toward blacks, there would have been the complicity of going along with racist customs, practices, and attitudes. This much active and passive racism among white people only meant that whites could be more credibly stigmatized as racists. It was the first time in all of American history that whites began to be truly accountable for their racism. And John, like millions of other baby boomers, launched his adolescent rebellion at the precise historical moment when all this came into play. In other words, baby boomers began to rebel just as white guilt emerged as one of greatest social, cultural, and political forces in all of American history.

I'm not with this guy

—any hippie
this also allowed for
people to stay in
their adolescee way into maturity.
I've done it, still doing this

13

ADOLESCENTS ALL

I remember a brief encounter I had with John during his dramatic return to campus. At a party he told me that if I really cared about civil rights, I too should head out to California. He said something about big things happening in the East Bay, as if I would certainly know where the East Bay was and what was happening there. I didn't know, or at least not until it was far too late to impress him with my up-to-the-minute command of the black protest scene. I just smiled, hoping he wouldn't notice the blank I was drawing, and waited for him to make his point. But there was to be no point. He took on the pained look of a man who would have loved to talk forever were it not for all the pressing calls on his time. He made a quick apology, and then he was gone. I never saw him again. Only later that night did I remember that the East Bay meant Oakland, California, the home of the Black Panthers.

But it was also surprising even to hear the words "civil rights" pass from John's lips. Like many young whites of that era, he seemed to have been untouched by racial matters. This was the first generation raised on TV and Disney, on sitcom images of an immaculately raceless America. Only the evening news, with its images of the civil rights struggle, gave most white children a window into the nation's "race problem." But this only made it a rather far-off and abstract "current event," something to be dutifully kept up with, and something therefore easily neglected. I would have been surprised if John even knew that there was a student civil rights group on our campus. Certainly racial injustice had nothing to do with the grand rebellion he was staging. And yet, the mere act of rebellion at that late sixties moment not only gained him an association with the great social issues of the day but also positioned him as a man of progressive sympathies, a man on the moral side of important issues.

This happened because John, I, and baby boomers generally were the beneficiaries of a near-perfect synchronicity between our adolescent rebellion and the advent of white guilt. We began to question adult authority at the precise historical moment when our parents began to lose moral authority to race, war, the women's issue, and so on. The adolescent rebel is always—at least secretly—a bit insecure, worrying on some level that his indictment of his parents might be wrong, fearing that they might in fact be better and more knowing people than he gives them credit for. This rebellion is normally more focused on achieving autonomy than on explicitly defeating one's parents. But for baby boomers, there was almost no way to avoid defeating them, no way to give the parental generation the benefit of the doubt. History itself seemed to have rendered a summary indictment against them. They were racist, sexist, militaristic, sexually repressed, hypocritical, shallow, "uptight," materialistic, chauvinistic, compassionless, and philistine. It was as if they had been called out, made to stand in military formation, and then frankly stripped of their authority before our very eyes.

The infamous "credibility gap" of that era between the government and its citizens, and the "generation gap" between the young and the old, were caused in part by this disgracing of adult authority. The old and powerful were not to be believed. And all of this was a formative, generation-defining experience for baby boomers, this witness to a far greater collapse of adult moral authority than previous generations had experienced. So, just as all the very normal tensions of youth roiled and built into something like a will—the adolescent will to individuate—we met an adult world so stripped of moral authority that it could not do the timeless work of adults, which is to say, "Here, and no further."

It was a strange experience to come of age in a society where most of what was familiar—the mainstream itself—lacked moral authority. This meant we were a generation that could not negotiate with the past, with traditions. We had to reject the past for its moral failings; therefore, we could not be reformers, only revolutionaries—thus our attraction to so many ideologies of revolution, so many ideas and faiths that flatly overturned what we were raised to believe. Mark Twain's quip simply did not apply to baby boomers. The foolish and morally compromised father that we knew at fourteen did not become brilliant and wise when we were nineteen. He remained foolish and was even more morally compromised than we had realized at fourteen, and it fell on us to make the world he had let down into a better place.

So this widening vacuum of moral authority in the adult world, this white guilt, constituted a default of adult authority that effectively put baby boomers in charge of redeeming America—of reinventing an America that would have moral authority in all the places where the "over thirties" had lost it. So, among other things, white guilt defined the overriding *social* responsibility of the baby-boom generation: to restore America's moral authority by tackling such issues as racial equality, international peace, and equality for women.

14

STUMBLING INTO POWER

None of this had yet become clear when John left our little college to answer the call of hippie life in California. And yet, John's surprising mention of civil rights and the East Bay shows me now that he had instinctively known enough to exploit the synchronicity between his personal act of rebellion and the default of adult authority. He would have known that his father was vulnerable to the charge of racism, that if racism was not a purple passion with his father, it was at least an unexamined predisposition, a habit of good manners—like taking one's hat off in the presence of ladies. He would have known, too, that his father's military background very likely made him a hawk on the war in Vietnam. Name the issue, and John, with reasonable confidence, could place his father on the wrong side of it. So whatever there was actually between them—the father's too narrow expectations, or John's unsuitability for college, or some other father-son grievance—would metamorphose from the personal to the political, where John could actually have *more* moral authority than his uptight father, who was implicated in so many social evils. Once on the political level, there would be a role reversal: the son would have the greater authority and the father would be on the defensive, arguing in support of a discredited "status quo" that had easily tolerated white male supremacy and American imperialism. The father would make a fat target for his son's sarcasm because even when he made good sense—demanding, say, that John finish college—his good sense would be bereft of moral authority. "Sure, I could finish college," John could say, "and join the racist, napalm-dropping, baby-killing establishment that you so love." John's father would have to answer his son from a great and deep hole dug by white guilt.

Wherever there is a vacuum of moral authority, there is inevitably a transfer of moral authority and, therefore, of power.

Thus it was that John—and baby boomers generally—happened onto possibly the greatest source of political, social, and cultural power in the late twentieth century: white guilt. This was the power—even the command—to invent America all over again in the interest of redeeming it. It was the power to transform every important institution and every area of society that had ever been touched by social injustice. And this included everything from the military to education, from the corporate world to the law, from voting rights to housing, from the practice of religion to the preservation of the environment. This was the power that launched the Great Society virtually overnight and that "integrated" public schools from Little Rock to Boston. It changed welfare into a socialism of guaranteed income and helped to ravage what had been the world's greatest public school system by battering it with decades of mindless, if well-intended, reforms.

And it transformed American citizens for both better and worse. It made whites understand that racism is evil, but it also coerced them right back into racial discrimination by miring the nation in the race-based "results" reforms of diversity and affirmative action. It seduced blacks into the self-destructive and ironic politics of militant dependency by encouraging a black identity of entitlement and grievance—an identity that produced a black leadership capable of little more than trading off moral authority to whites and American institutions for racial preferences.

If you think of all the ways that white racism affected and controlled American life before the sixties—from the ugly customs of a segregated society, to the private bigotry that propped up the identities of millions of whites, to the power of racism to stigmatize both blacks and whites—that will be a good measure of the scope and power of white guilt in American life since the sixties. Like racism, white guilt not only generates new social customs, redefines the way institutions function, gives us new law, and reorients our national politics; it also, in a sense, makes a new world by forever altering our idea of virtue. It says that white supremacy is not a moral truth that decency requires us to observe, but rather an evil that decency requires us to condemn. This new virtue demands that whites condemn the idea of their own racial superiority. So white guilt means that white skin now *subtracts* moral authority from rather than adds it to people and, thus, imposes humility where it once granted superiority.

White guilt is essentially a historical force that follows naturally from a moral evolution in a specific society. Thus, it is implacable. It remakes the world as profoundly, and as awkwardly, as the immorality it overthrows once did.

15

THE END OF WHITE SUPREMACY

White guilt was the enormous source of power that John and other baby-boomer rebels found themselves carried forward on, as if a great gravitational pull were bearing them into a future entirely of their own making. In a reminiscence of his time in the sixties within the orbit of the writer and sixties icon Ken Kesey (the subject of Tom Wolfe's New Journalism classic *The Electric Kool-Aid Acid Test*), the novelist Robert Stone says: "More than the inhabitants of any other decade before us, we believed ourselves in a time of our own making." Elsewhere he describes himself and Kesey enjoying one of the sixties' more notorious pastimes—on the bank of a creek in the soft coastal mountains above Palo Alto they shared a joint. "We sat and smoked and possibility came down on us."

Possibility coming down like a kind of rain. Living in "a time of our own making." These were the new promises that the sixties made to our generation, and these promises imbued John with a certain charisma during his brief return to campus. He had attached himself to a new unfolding history and crossed out of our mundane world of eight o'clock chem labs and work-study jobs. With him all was suddenly numinous and poignantly possible.

It would be overreaching to suggest that white guilt was the only historical force behind all this—behind not only John as an augur of things to come but also the social, cultural, and generational transformations that began in the sixties. Certainly each transformation had its own source and logic and history—feminism, for example. And yet, I would argue that white guilt—this unforeseen diminution of moral authority that came after the open acknowledgment of racial wrongdoing—was a far more powerful force than commonly assumed. This is so because it replaced one of the greatest sources of "moral" authority in the history of the modern world: white supremacy.

This was the authority that had given white America the hubris to live rather easily with slavery and segregation even as these practices glaringly violated every principle the nation was founded on. White supremacy—commonly accepted as a *moral* truth about the world, as a fact of nature reflecting God's intended hierarchy of races—gave whites the moral authority to exclude other races from the American democracy as inferiors. This was also the authority that justified European colonialism as a "white man's burden." Though this specious claim of innate superiority is a human impulse present in all races, it has been a special problem in the Western world because it is supported by a very visible and real superiority of wealth and power. The dangerous logic is very simple: if whites have more power than others, they must also have an innate superiority over others—the former proving the latter.

But the clearest and most important implication of the great acknowledgment was that superior power is not the same thing as innate superiority, and that being in an inferior position is not the same thing as being innately inferior. The white Western world (like other dominant cultures in history) had often muddied this distinction precisely to grant itself an illicit authority over nonwhites in inferior positions. The whole point of racism (and sexism, anti-Semitism, etc.) is to seize authority illicitly at the expense of another race. The racist says, "My God-given superiority *is* my authority, so my domination of inferiors is in God's plan. What I think is *conclusive*, and what I say determines the course of things because God and nature want it so." Nazis acted against Jews on the authority of their God-given Aryan superiority. Whites segregated blacks in America on the authority of God's gift to them of superiority. When America admitted racial wrongdoing and passed strong civil rights legislation in the sixties, it delegitimized exactly this kind of authority—authority justified by an assertion that God made your group superior to all others.

But how did the delegitimizing of white supremacy expand white guilt? The answer begins in what replaced white supremacy: the view that white Western supremacy came not from an innate racial superiority but from an innate capacity for evil, that the wealth and power of whites did not prove God's favoritism for them but rather proved their special talent for dehumanizing others on a grand scale—their will to go forth and dominate others; to steal resources; to enslave, to conquer, to convert, to exploit, to exclude, and even to annihilate others. So white supremacy was replaced, in its same proportion, by the idea of white evil. And this was a profound change for America and the West because white supremacy had been a great source of *authority,* and thus a license and a power to act without serious regard for nonwhites.

I remember a tense interaction with my seventh-grade history teacher, the indomitable Mrs. Burgess, that illustrates the near-perfect invisibility—and thus the power—of white supre-macy as a source of authority. It was the late fifties. America was still ensconced in its long age of racism, so my parents had had to finagle and sacrifice to get me into an all-white junior high school, where they hoped I would get the kind of education that segregation reserved for whites. So, moving from an all-black segregated school, I suddenly found myself the lone black in a classroom of white faces. But I got along well, made good friends, and began to recover from the years of academic blight I had endured in my old segregated school.

Still, one day in American history class, we came to a moment that I had long been dreading. Our American history textbook, which to my great relief skimmed over the entire subject of slavery in mere paragraphs, included—as if in a cruelty meant especially for me—the photograph of a slave woman standing in a cotton field in a ragged and shapeless dress, her head bound in an Aunt Jemima bandanna as if to cover the indecency of her hair, her eyes fat and round and bulging, her thick lips pushed into a grotesque smile of doglike happiness. Today I would place this photograph in the Diane Arbus school of photography, where the art is in the bravery of unsparingly photographing the face of human inferiority. But I was twelve and the only black in the class, and there was no art for me in this photograph. There was only mortification and dread of the day when the class would come to this brief slavery section and everyone's book would open to the page with this misbegotten, dehumanized creature, and the whole class would look over at me.

The day came. I was mortified. The class indeed looked my way or, worse, looked down in embarrassment for me. The caption beneath the picture was our lesson for the day: that American slaves worked hard but were well cared for and were, therefore, a happy people that liked to dance and sing—like the happy woman in the picture. At home I had been primed to speak up politely at such moments, to try to make a point, if I could, and then to let it rest. In the age of racism, America's oppression of blacks had not yet been officially acknowledged, so blacks had no special moral authority that whites recognized. White supremacy meant the reverse: that whites were entitled to ignore black complaint and protest without penalty. So even the most polite objections by blacks invited the "troublemaker" label.

Still, in class discussion I managed to mumble something to the effect that I didn't think the slaves had been entirely happy. Mrs. Burgess, a kind if stern woman with a rolling eye, ignored me so utterly that I began to wonder if she had heard me at all. Minutes passed before I realized that my little comment was going to disappear into the ether. Hours later that same day she stopped me in the hallway. Finally, I thought, I will get my response, even if it will now be between only the two of us. But she only reminded me about something mundane that I was supposed to do, like patrol-boy duty. I must have shown a little disappointment, which finally brought the flicker of recognition I had been hoping for. I could virtually see her remembering my little dissent, but as she did, her look turned to hard irritability. Clearly, she wanted me to see that I was pushing her too far, that if I was going to start making little racial protests, her magnanimity would soon be exhausted. Everything about her said that she was doing me a favor by not holding my dissent against me, and that she expected me to be grateful. I got the point and smiled, making it clear that I wanted no trouble. She smiled back, her rolling eye ambling off on its own. And that was it. Neither she nor I nor anyone else mentioned the subject of slavery again.

Was Mrs. Burgess a white supremacist?

No, I don't believe so. Mrs. Burgess's worldview—formed in the first half of the twentieth century—may have been informed by ignorances and stereotypes that would easily qualify her as a racist today. But she was essentially a kind person and no part of her self-esteem seemed propped up by racial animus. Still, like all white teachers in those days, she was imbued with an *authority* that came from white supremacy. I have little doubt that she saw the idea of happy slaves as ridiculous. But in those areas where a society is repressed, so that even obvious truths are explosive, people often go along with the ridiculous as the least of many evils. Mrs. Burgess was not going to open the can of worms I wanted to open, and in that age of racism she had the authority not to. She was going to maintain the *propriety* of white supremacy, which made truth in the matter of slavery an impropriety. And also in this context, she was trying to save me from myself. She believed, as I did, that the age of racism would continue indefinitely. I would have to live in it, and she wanted me to know that this sort of challenging attitude would not work no matter what my parents—known troublemakers—had told me.

So it was out of a certain human kindness—even affection—that Mrs. Burgess had ignored my comment. She knew that we would both live under the *authority* of white supremacy no matter what we thought of white supremacy itself. And she wanted me to learn how to live with that authority. But more important, she was utterly secure in her authority to teach me this lesson. In that age of racism, her judgment in racial matters had authority even though—and especially because—she was white. So all that year she would watch me and then, in some quiet and private way, let me know what she thought. After a basketball game in which I fouled out early, she let me know the next day that it wasn't good for the only black on the floor to commit so many fouls. "People will think the wrong thing." Her comments were made quickly, often in passing, and they were never open for discussion.

Today Mrs. Burgess would be seen as an enforcer of racial hierarchy because she was essentially an accommodationist: someone who showed kindness to blacks by helping them accommodate to white supremacy. And shouldn't her kindness have gone into combating white supremacy? Maybe so, but this is a little like glibly passing judgment on someone who learns to survive under a totalitarian regime. White supremacy was the authority we were both accountable to, and though today Mrs. Burgess could easily be judged an accommodationist, back then I thought of her only as a kind of friend.

Nevertheless, it was a mere ten years later that I stood in Dr. McCabe's office—with a full beard and an Afro approaching the size of a healthy yard shrub—defiantly spilling cigarette ashes onto the carpet and reading out a list of demands. Mrs. Burgess would surely have disapproved. And I cannot imagine her ever restraining herself in the way that Dr. McCabe restrained himself. But then I cannot imagine her outside her full authority, a part of which came from white supremacy. But for Dr. McCabe this source of authority was already fast disappearing. I met him after America's great acknowledgment, thus after the idea of evil had begun to attach to America and to whites. All around him, like an aura, was the specter of white moral inferiority, of American moral cowardice. White supremacy had been Mrs. Burgess's aura and a very important source of her incontestable authority. But this same white supremacy later robbed Dr. McCabe of authority. Not only did he put up with behavior that Mrs. Burgess would never have tolerated, but he took up many of our demands, silly as they were, and implemented them— as did countless other college presidents across the country. It wasn't just that he had lost the authority of white supremacy, that special grace that whiteness bestowed. But that grace had become a disgrace, a shame that weakened his authority to the point where he found himself appeasing black students who were asking for utterly absurd things simply to feel the power that white guilt had opened to them.

And so the delegitimizing of white supremacy greatly expanded white guilt because it turned an authority asset into an authority deficit by linking white supremacy more to a capacity for evil than to innate racial superiority. It created a new moral/racial iconography in which whiteness became more an icon of racial evil than of racial supremacy. One part of white guilt is the horrible moral hypocrisy of racism in a democracy, of loving freedom and then denying it to nonwhites. The other part is the claim of innate white superiority as a justification for this hypocrisy and as a license to commit evil against racial inferiors. Once acknowledged, as happened in the mid-sixties, this legacy of hypocrisy and evil simply began to corrode the moral authority of whites.

Some long-simmering power that had always been weakly alive beneath the repressions of white supremacy had finally broken through and won its point, so that traditional America could never again see itself as an innocent society, as a straightforward society of honest, optimistic, ingenious, and freedom-loving whites.

16

A COHERENCE GONE OUT OF THE WORLD

So the vivid sense of possibility that young baby boomers walked into in the early sixties—which opened the way for the coming counterculture—came to them through the death of white authority, the authority that white skin itself had always carried in America. Possibility was a positive fallout of this death, but there was also another, more ambiguous fallout. When white supremacy was delegitimized so that common decency required Americans to treat it as a great evil, all whites lost the right to any racial self-consciousness. In other words, they lost the right to a *white* identity. Whites cannot celebrate their race without aligning themselves with white supremacy and, thus, with the murder, enslavement, and exploitation of millions the world over. This prohibition is a feature of their lost moral authority, another element or territory of white guilt.

In fact, if there is a white racial identity today it would have to be white guilt—a shared, even unifying, lack of racial moral authority. As other group identities derive from a shared fate, white guilt is a shared white fate rendered up by history. Whites can no more escape white guilt than blacks can reject being black—the latter cannot know themselves *racially* without the memory of slavery, and the former cannot know themselves *racially* without the memory of white supremacy. Two shaming fates, yes, but two identities? Can an identity revolve around contrition and deference toward darker races, as a modern white identity would have to? Does it make sense for whites to go around saying, "We are the contrite people, and we defer to other races; this is our identity"? Yet to gain employment today in most American institutions whites must somehow pledge allegiance to "diversity" as if to demonstrate a white identity of contrition and deference. Even in the corporate and military worlds—not to mention academia—no white goes far without genuflecting to diversity. Nevertheless, beyond an identity that apologizes for white supremacy, absolutely no white identity is permissible.

But isn't this a good thing? Aren't America and the Western world—if not the entire world—already much better off now that whites are denied white supremacy and any form of racial identity outside contrition?

It is very easy to be morally glib about this, to see the loss of white authority only in relation to an idea of justice, and thus to say that it was entirely a good thing and overdue to boot. It was a good thing, and it was overdue. But the death of white authority also meant that something culturally enormous— something that had brought great cohesion and coherence to society—began to go out of the world. If white Western societies were racist and imperialistic, they were also the centers of an indisputably great civilization (one that absorbed contributions from many other races and cultures). But when white supremacy was delegitimized, whites did not simply lose the authority to practice racism. The loss of authority generalized well beyond that, so that whites also lost a degree of their authority to stand proudly for the values and ideas that had made the West a great civilization despite its many evils.

This points to a fundamental problem with moral authority, whether in societies, institutions, or individuals: it is absolutely necessary because it bestows legitimacy on the exercise of power, but it generalizes too easily, often granting more legitimacy than it should to those who have moral authority, and denying more legitimacy than it should to those who don't have it. When white supremacy was itself a source of moral authority, Western societies felt nothing less than an extravagant legitimacy, ranging over the entire earth, taking what they wanted, even "depopulating" many regions of "inferiors." The authority derived from their presumed innate superiority made whites gods of the earth whose every base instinct for plunder, rape, and systematic oppression could be *legitimately* indulged. But without white supremacy as a source of moral authority, the reverse began to happen. The loss of moral authority went too far the other way, not only denying legitimacy to the plunder of the nonwhite world but also denying it to that entire set of difficult "character" principles that bring coherence and even greatness to free societies: personal responsibility, hard work, individual initiative, delayed gratification, commitment to excellence, competition by merit, the honor in achievement, and so on. How could these principles be important when they had coexisted so easily with racism? Weren't they, in fact, a part of the machinery of white supremacy?

In the age of racism, blacks were held accountable to these values and principles even though they were also openly oppressed. Therefore, there was a cultural coherence in America based on these values and principles that applied to *everybody* despite the presence of segregation. This coherence, in itself, was a good thing, and was surely responsible for much that was great in the character of white and black Americans. Moreover, it might have provided an ideal consensus of values out of which to build a post-white supremacy society. But the delegitimization of white supremacy greatly injured this cultural coherence by taking authority away from the values and principles it was based on. After America admitted to what was worst about itself, there was not enough authority left to support what was best.

THE WAYS OF BLINDNESS

Personal Responsibility
Hard work
individual initiative
delayed gratification
commitment to excellence
competition by merit
~~the~~ honor in achievement

17

A CONTINGENT POWER

At last I turned off Highway 101 just before the city of Salinas and headed due west on Highway 68 toward the Monterey Peninsula and the cool Pacific. It was still a sunny and clear winter day, which meant there would be no fog over the coast to smother the sun. In summer the ocean fog—sucked over land by hot air from the central valley—could greet you many miles inland from the coast, and almost immediately the world would be gray and seasonless and the air would be thirty degrees cooler. But this winter day my trip into Monterey and home would be sunny all the way.

My only worry was that home would come too quickly. I wanted at least some resolution of the little Clinton-Eisenhower dilemma I had posed for myself that morning. At home there would be distractions. It had been a luxury just to drive along in Chautauqua-like contemplation of a paradox: why it was that each of these presidents would very likely lose office for committing the other's sin but not for committing his own sin. The luxury had been the fullness of time, the empty hours in which to let experience and idea build on each other—and to experience the landscape as a kind of friend to thought. In mythology journeys always end in epiphany or knowledge or resonant meaning.

I didn't think my little trip would clear any of these hurdles, but I wasn't ready for it to end, and there were still a few hours of daylight left in the sky. So just where the vast fields west of Salinas came to an end, and where the rolling coastal mountains began, I pulled off the highway and into Toro Canyon Park. In minutes I was hiking slowly up a gently rising trail at the bottom of a deep canyon. I knew the trail well but appointed myself no destination, no time frame. Even if darkness caught me I would know my way out. So very soon I once again had the feeling that time was on my side.

And it was out of this feeling that it occurred to me that Bill Clinton had truly benefited from white guilt, that it was responsible for the new idea of virtue that was keeping him in office. And this notion of virtue was a very specific response to a very specific problem: the problem of having great power but not a commensurate authority.

The great acknowledgment had diminished the moral authority of whites but not their power or the degree of their responsibility for society. Whites continued to run America in every way after owning up to racism. This meant that whites, American institutions, and the American democracy itself began to run at a conspicuous deficit of legitimacy. Even the individual white who had lifted himself from poverty to great success could not say that simply being white had not helped him. Thus, in his success there was a tincture of illegitimacy.

So America's great acknowledgment did not cause power to change hands directly from one race to another, but it did make the power that whites wield in society a *contingent power*—a power that must satisfy certain social or moral contingencies before it can be considered legitimate. After the mid-sixties, power exercised by whites, in the public and private sectors, had to *dissociate* from the sins that had caused whites to lose moral authority in the first place—racism and racial discrimination but also imperialism, ecological indifference, sexism, and so on.

President Johnson's Great Society, for example, was created—above all else—to meet this new contingency of *dissociating* American power from the nation's racist past. American legitimacy was the Great Society's most important purpose. And it achieved this purpose through a dissociation from the ill will toward blacks that had characterized all of American history. The Great Society was essentially an apology for the racism that had made the American democracy illegitimate. And its true purpose was not to "end poverty in our time," but to restore legitimacy to the American democracy.

More recently the three branches of the American military submitted a brief to the Supreme Court in the University of Michigan affirmative-action case arguing that they needed to use racial preferences for the sake of troop morale. Given the large number of minority recruits, they claimed to need more minority officers. And in order to achieve this they needed to be able to lower standards for minorities. I do not believe for a second that there is any sound military reason for engineering parity between minority officers and minority recruits at the expense of better-qualified people. Certainly minorities, like whites, deserve to be led by the best available officers rather than by officers of their own race. Double standards *always* stigmatize precisely those they claim to help, so it will be minority officers—not white officers—who will be seen as second-rate under such a system.

But, of course, troop morale is no more than a rationalization *by whites* for the social engineering they must do for their own legitimacy. Are we to believe that the morale of young whites is improved when they must work their way up the ranks in a system stacked against them? The military is simply an American institution, and its legitimacy is contingent on an explicit dissociation from racism. Yet a fair application of merit would disproportionately favor whites and therefore seem a continuance of the racist past rather than a break from it. No moral authority here, no legitimacy, only a vulnerability to charges of racism. So the hard reality of a skill disparity between the races must be engineered around, not for minorities, who end up stigmatized and with no better skills, but for the legitimacy of the institution. Likewise, when President Bush proclaims his faith in "diversity" and brags about the "diversity" of his cabinet, he is really only arguing that he has satisfied the contingency that makes his possession of power legitimate.

18

BLAMELESS POVERTY

Not many years ago I met a man at a conference who said he had been an "architect" of President Johnson's Great Society. I was standing in a small clump of people at a conference reception when I noticed him looking at me out of dark and frankly glaring eyes. I could see that he had business with me. When he introduced himself, I thought I ever so vaguely recognized his name, but in fact I didn't. I felt guilty that I couldn't recall the name of an "architect" of the Great Society.

He had read something I'd written that was critical of the Great Society, and he said bluntly that it bothered him. Then he paused, collecting himself as if what he had to say was too important to utter in anger. In measured tones he explained that he had not gone into government intending to help build the Great Society. "You never know what's going to land in your lap when you're in government." But he and the others in the Johnson administration had done the best they could in a "difficult situation." Now, decades later, he realized there had been many problems, but he thought there was also much to be proud of. "Don't you give us credit for anything?" he asked. And it was a good question. I had given some years of my own life to Great Society programs. Had those years finally added up to nothing?

Before I could answer he began to describe for me what it had been like back then, as this great social experiment had unfolded. And here he was softened by a tone of nostalgia, an older man recalling a golden age. They had wanted, very literally, to invent a new society, he said, to do something extraordinary and grand. Then, with an ironic smile, he uttered that age's great cliché: "to end poverty in our own time." They had been true believers. And they had had the *power* of the United States government, the wealthiest and most powerful government in the entire world, to work with—billions of dollars and, if not a clear mandate, at least a certain political momentum coming off the passage of the 1964 Civil Rights Act.

But for me the Great Society had been more a dark age than a golden one. By the time I got to East St. Louis in 1968 I had already worked in two programs—one in rural Iowa, one in Minneapolis—but East St. Louis was of a different order. This small, and almost entirely black, city was famous as what was once called a "black bottom." On Thanksgiving morning I heard loud voices and looked out the kitchen window to see our neighbor shooting at his teenage son with a pistol, grazing the boy's stomach. Weeks later, walking into a convenience store one block from our apartment, I saw a dead body lying at the foot of a Dumpster, dressed in a sharkskin suit, impeccable in every detail except for the seepings of blood that left beet-colored stains on the shiny cloth. One of my best students—bright, well loved, college-bound, and a bit of a nerd whose innocence had been preserved by a devoted mother who had ensconced him in the sanctuary of the black church—was shot dead standing outside a teenage house party in a gang drive-by. The brilliant "cool" kid in the program, the urban equivalent of the suburban homecoming king, was shot to death beneath a viaduct near the Mississippi River for trying to move in on the local drug trade. Other boys came back from juvenile hall wearing lipstick and earrings. East St. Louis foreshadowed the welfare-gang-drug culture that was soon to infuse one urban ghetto after another, and so it qualified for virtually every Great Society program there was.

The Great Society presented itself to East St. Louis primarily as money—money given in the name of black poverty but with no real accountability for being effective against poverty. Thus it engendered a kind of "upscale" corruption in which money changed hands and the government was told what it wanted to hear: that because we were black we *knew* the people we were working with, and because we were "innovative," we had the magic to steer them out of poverty. All we needed was more money, always more money.

In fact, we did not know what we were doing. "Innovation" was simply a mantra we took up as a license to entertain all manner of gimcrack educational ideas, the "beauty" of which was that they always promised to let us achieve great things by demanding less of our students and of ourselves. We talked of "black ways of knowing," which, of course, effectively gave all black teachers a kind of racial teaching credential that whites could never have. We devalued rigorous academic work by insisting that black students learned "experientially" and "intuitively," and by arguing that "street knowledge" was often more valuable than "book" knowledge. There were certainly exceptions to all of this, people who worked earnestly with their students and taught substantive classes. But these serious people found themselves in an atmosphere of black excuse-making and incompetence, and they quickly left.

So the program began to decline almost as soon as it began, yet it burned through as much government money as it possibly could, increased its budget requests each year, and constantly developed specialized proposals for even more money. (One such proposal brought us the services of an itinerant psychologist, an attractive blond woman who came by a few times a week to provide often rather noisy closed-door sessions to several of our male students.) Factions developed as better people left and as those left behind vied for their positions and money. There were occasions when people appeared at staff meetings with weapons conspicuously outlined under their clothes. So, finally, the two worlds of corruption—the street world of gangs and drug lords, and the poverty-program world of abundant government money—began to merge.

This program, like so many others in that era, failed because it operated out of a new definition of poverty, one born of the impossible constraint that white guilt imposed on the exercise of government power where race and poverty were concerned.

This was the new definition of poverty that led to the excoriation of Daniel Patrick Moynihan in 1965. As assistant secretary of labor, Moynihan had presumed that he had the authority—if not a responsibility—to look frankly at black poverty. And his study, *The Negro Family: The Case for National Action*, offered a description of black poverty that history has now shown to have been amazingly prescient. There is no longer serious debate among scholars on Moynihan's broad finding— that children from single-parent, female-headed households have more, and more serious, problems than do children from two-parent homes. But Moynihan had not accounted for the ascendance of white guilt and for the fact that his white skin— once a source of impunity—now robbed him of authority in racial matters. Nor could he have realized in 1965 that he was working for a government with power but little authority around race. In this context, whites simply could not criticize black life without being seen as racist, no matter what their intentions were. His fine study immediately became an untouchable document in both government and academia. He was made an object lesson for America's intellectual class: castigation and disregard await all white scholars who see black poverty outside a context of victimization.

But more important, Moynihan's fate marked the end of white America's authority over the problems of inequality and poverty, problems for which it nevertheless retained responsibility. Since the sixties, poverty has been defined in America not by its reality but out of the squeeze of a double bind: responsibility without authority. Thus, poverty came to be seen as a condition unrelated to the dysfunctions of those who suffer it, and always treatable by the "interventions" of government and other institutions. With this "blameless" poverty (poverty that never "blames the victim"), the government can be responsible for poverty even as it lacks authority over it. And responsibility is all the government needs, because therein lies the moral authority and legitimacy it seeks. So "blameless" poverty is no more than a white ingenuity which allows institutions to steal responsibility for a problem they lack the authority to even honestly define.

Nevertheless, it is an ingenuity that brings real power to whites who embrace it. But it is not the responsibility for poverty that really matters; what matters is that responsibility brings legitimacy. And if you can restore legitimacy to American institutions in this age of white guilt, then you have real power. This has been the essential power of the political left in America since the sixties—this promise to restore legitimacy by taking responsibility for inequality and poverty even though there is no authority to define these problems accurately. What all this boils down to is that black poverty—of the kind I encountered in East St. Louis—became a currency of legitimacy (and power) for the government, the political left, and American institutions. The only catch was that those who suffered poverty had to be utterly blameless so that responsibility (legitimacy and power) would automatically fall to whites.

19

WHITE BLINDNESS

Clearly the man who introduced himself to me as an "architect" of the Great Society saw nothing cynical in what he and his fellow architects had done in the sixties. He was quite proud of the effort they had made. "And I'll tell you something else," he said, his fierce black eyes boring into me, "we just needed to keep at it. We were learning new things all the time, but then the war took all the money away, and, you're right, things did sort of go to hell after that, but . . ."

"What kind of things did you learn that would have helped all those programs do better?"

"Look," he said irritably, "*only*—and I mean *only*—the government can get to that kind of poverty, that entrenched, deep poverty. And I don't care what you say. If this country was decent, it would let the government try again."

"But what did you learn from all those programs and all that money spent?"

But then he only wanted to tell stories—a trip he had taken

to the Mississippi Delta, the gratitude of the people for a local VISTA program, the "new hope" they had taken from seeing their government caring about them. I told him I had heard the same gratitude countless times in the programs I had worked in, but there were tough questions to be asked. If so many people were grateful and newly hopeful, why didn't they build on what they had been given and continue to improve themselves after the programs dried up? Why did so many just hold out for welfare or merely plod along as before? Why wasn't there a better use of the public schools, a demand that they teach at a higher level? Why not private schools in basements and churches? Why not simple credit unions to provide capital? (My own father had started one in the segregated neighborhood where I grew up. My mother had organized a free baby clinic.) Why inertia instead of an energized focus on all the new possibilities that the civil rights victories had opened up? And finally, if the Great Society was so good, why did black America produce its first true underclass *after* it was over?

"Damn it, we *saved* this country!" he all but shouted. "This country was about to blow up. There were riots everywhere. You can stand there now in hindsight and criticize, but we had to keep the country together, my friend."

"That's my point," I said. "The Negroes you met in the Mississippi Delta were a means to your end."

"They were no goddamn means to any end. I will never forget those people. If the government had stayed there, we would have saved them."

I tried to explain about white guilt, moral authority, and legitimacy, but it was no use. Exasperated, he turned sharply and walked away; then he turned again and came back. His anger had given way to a cold contempt, and his black eyes were dull now, almost gray. "I'm telling you, we saved this country and you need to appreciate that."

I had met a few others like him, men who had been in on the ground floor of important racial policies back in the sixties and seventies, like school busing, various Great Society programs, and affirmative action. They were a touchy lot, and I could understand why. For one thing, they were victims of what historians call "presentism"—having their past innovations constantly judged in the light of present-day standards and with all the smugness of hindsight. Policies that had once seemed destined to deliver America from centuries of racial shame were now seen through the prism of decades of failure and cultural divisiveness. The innovators themselves—men who once heroically challenged America's moral inertia around race—found themselves now associated with all this failure rather than with the glory of past good intentions.

One such man that I knew wrote eloquently on what America was like back then, on how racial discrimination—an entrenched practice that gave millions of unskilled whites an economic advantage over blacks—had still prevailed everywhere in America in the late sixties, and on how his innovative policies had broken up many of these enclaves of white privilege. His subtext was that he had done a good thing, and if the policy he had created to breach white privilege had turned out to be disastrous over time and in other contexts, then that in no way mitigated the good he had done. It must also be added to the credit of such men that they had often faced down open racists, as President Johnson himself had done in his negotiations over the 1964 Civil Rights Bill when he told his old friend and mentor, Sam Rayburn, that things were going to change.

And yet these men were also victims of another, far more common human problem: they did not entirely know themselves (like most of us), which often left them blind to their actual motivations. Most any time race is given importance, positively or negatively, people are hiding from their true motivations. In the age of racism, whites said blacks were inferior so as not to *see* their own desire to exploit them, their true motivation. In the age of white guilt, whites support all manner of silly racial policies without seeing that their true motivation is simply to show themselves innocent of racism.

The theme of white blindness is one of the most persistent themes in twentieth-century writing by black Americans— blindness toward others but, more important, toward the self. The essence of this theme is that whites have always had to nurture a certain blindness toward themselves in order to preserve their moral character in a racist society that favors them, and that this nurtured blindness is a part of the American culture, a part of what it means to be white in America. Thus, the blindness of whites to their true motivations in racial matters is a rather timeless feature of American life, as visible in today's university president rationalizing affirmative action as it was in Thomas Jefferson's last rationalizations for the continuance of slavery. In both cases, a white man argues out of a humanity that is aloof and God-graced for a race-based system that will utterly define black life, but that he himself will never be subject to. That whites can devise and support such systems while being blind to their true motivations is a special terror in black life, one that is explored in the work of Richard Wright, James Baldwin, Chester Himes, and many other black writers. It is always the black who pays the price for white self-delusion. And it is always blacks who will have to seek out their opportunities—like Odysseus against the Cyclops—within the blindness of whites. Whites, on the other hand—today's college president, yesterday's Thomas Jefferson—not only will never suffer from the systems they devise, but will be forever celebrated for their good intentions, their courage in confronting such an intractable problem.

The majority decision of the Supreme Court in the recent University of Michigan affirmative-action case is an especially insensitive example of white blindness, every bit as chilling and bizarre as the contorted mathematical calculations by which Thomas Jefferson tried to figure out the number of years it would take to ship all slaves back to Africa—calculations which so defeated him that he finally ended his lifelong wrestling with the slavery issue by ceding the problem to future generations. The odd reasoning of Justice Sandra Day O'Connor's majority opinion in the Michigan case has the same myopic and abstracted quality as Jefferson's machinations. In a borrowed psuedoscientific doublespeak—"learning outcomes," "soft variables," "selection index," "nuanced judgments," "critical mass," and "holistic reading"—O'Connor piles one social-science banality on top of another, hoping against hope that we buy her tall tale of "diversity" as so "compelling" a state interest that it justifies racial preferences. Her opaque language is a textbook illustration of George Orwell's famous critique of political language as words used to "obscure" and hide reality rather than to illuminate it.

So in thrall is she to a soulless and undefined "diversity" that she ignores the most basic legal issues in the case: the constitutionality of preferring one race over another, as well as the court's careful precedents on racial preferences—"narrow tailoring" and "strict construction."

But more important, Justice O'Connor shows no interest in *seeing* the real causes of racial inequality in college admissions. She never identifies an actual problem that black students are having in college admissions that might be remedied by racial preferences. As always with white blindness, blacks and other minorities are invisible *as human beings*. So O'Connor never matches a problem that minorities are experiencing as human beings with a remedy.

This points to the shocking irony that defines her decision and renders it absurd: she applies a remedy to something that is not a problem—diversity. Diversity, of course, is not unfairness, discrimination, or a systemic bias that disproportionately hurts minorities. To the contrary, diversity is put forth as a social good, something on the positive side of the ledger. So O'Connor is saying that it is perfectly constitutional to have a remedy that remediates nothing, a race-based remedy that does not remediate racial discrimination; and that this is so even when that remedy is literally executed through programmatic racial discrimination.

But why is this an example of white blindness? And what specifically is white blindness? It is a blindness to the *human* reality of minorities that occurs when whites look at racial issues but see only the contingency they must meet to restore their own moral authority. White blindness is an unconscious self-absorption by which whites see racial issues—and even interracial encounters—as opportunities to dissociate from historic racism. Thus, encountering the black face is more an opportunity to dissociate than to see a human being like oneself. This is blindness because it confuses the mere dissociation from racism with sight, with seeing the human reality of racially different people. The two are not the same. To see humanity across racial lines one must see frankly how people of other races live as human beings, not as members of a race.

As mentioned earlier, over one hundred American institutions—universities, corporations, the military, state and local governments—submitted briefs to the Supreme Court in the Michigan case supporting racial preferences. Yet, despite all this commitment to diversity and racial preferences, I am not aware of a single institution that based its call for preferences on a careful analysis of why so many minorities were not competitive enough to win places in their institutions unaided by racial preferences. Again, if we can't specifically name the problems that make so many minorities noncompetitive, how can we argue that racial preferences are a remedy?

But, of course, these institutions are not interested in the reasons for minority noncompetitiveness; they are interested only in the *fact* that this persistent weakness means they must use preferences to rope in enough minorities. And what is enough minorities? Enough is just enough to clearly *dissociate* the institution from America's old racist patterns. Without preferences it would be utterly impossible to admit enough minorities for a convincing dissociation. Dissociation requires evidence of a proactive effort, a self-conscious and highly visible *display* of minority recruitment that shows the institution to be actively at war with its racist past. Thus, to conspicuously dissociate, it should be clear that preferences *were* used.

Most Ivy League universities want their freshmen classes to be roughly 8 percent black. This works as dissociation because they would be no more than 1 or 2 percent black without racial preferences. Eight percent verifies proactive effort because, at the very least, it quadruples the number of blacks that would otherwise be there. This, really, is the meaning of the infamous terms "quotas" and "quota system," terms that can be understood only in the language of white guilt. A "quota" is simply the percentage of minorities required to verify proactive minority recruitment in a given institution—minority recruitment at a level that sacrifices the institution's integrity, its timeless standards, and its fairness to whites and Asians. Lower standards and collateral discrimination—these are the tests of dissociation. And once dissociated, the institution goes about its business without worrying why minorities do so poorly within it.

20

WHITE BLINDNESS AND SAMBO

By far the best literary depiction of white blindness ever written has to be the "Mr. Norton" episode in Ralph Ellison's classic 1953 novel, *Invisible Man*. This episode is a virtual allegory of white blindness in which the invisible man—the novel's young black protagonist—ends up being kicked out of college because he lacks the time-honored black skill of manipulating white blindness. Dr. Bledsoe, the president of this college based on the real Tuskegee Institute in Alabama, tells him just before sending him away, "Every nigger in the cotton patch knows you're suppose to lie to a white man." And this is precisely what the invisible man failed to do as he toured the pompous and self-absorbed Mr. Norton around the campus. Norton is a wealthy white philanthropist from the North who contributes lavishly to this small black college in response to the soaring rhetoric of Dr. Bledsoe—a man who has crafted his "lies" to the white using blacks for ar own personal salvation.

man into a perfect moneymaking mask. In his sermons Bledsoe essentially presents the striving black race as an opportunity for white transcendence. By contributing to his college, whites can dissociate from the devastation racism has wrought on blacks. They can tell themselves that their contributions so improve the lives of blacks that they are effectively rendering racism benign. So Bledsoe, making his way in an openly racist society, sells whites a kind of absolution, a renewed sense of moral authority as they live out lives that are unavoidably complicit with racism.

But the invisible man threatens to crack Bledsoe's carefully constructed mask when he unthinkingly allows Norton to meet the rough-hewn black sharecropper Trueblood, who has—to the outrage of both black and white communities—impregnated both his wife and his daughter. Trueblood (a name symbolizing the unvarnished lower-class Negro) represents precisely the dark, messy, and fallen *human* reality of black life that Bledsoe labors so hard to keep hidden. Bledsoe offers up his people as innocents, as simple, almost childlike people who, without guile or resentment toward their oppressors, strive to live by an American ethic of hard, honorable work and humble hope. It is a vision of the Negro as a kind of pet, a figure of sweet and harmless inferiority to whom one gives out of the largesse of one's superiority. So Bledsoe throws the invisible man out of his college for being "dangerous," for allowing a white man *with money* to look behind the black mask and see the human frailty, and even Oedipal complexity, of black people—and all the more dangerous because Norton has unknowingly revealed an unnatural obsession with his own daughter.

Bledsoe's panicky fear is that the Trueblood encounter will

give *sight* to Norton, an ability to see past the delusion of race and into the human reality of blacks—and perhaps even to experience a human brotherhood with them. This possibility is simply too dangerous for Bledsoe even to contemplate, because he has predicated all his advantage on white blindness, on the easy gratification he can offer whites by giving them the opportunity to help inferiors, people who will be forever beneath them.

Norton's own unacknowledged incestuous impulse is a *human*—not a racial—link to Trueblood. It is only Norton's blindness to blacks as human beings—despite all the money he gives to their cause—that saves him from seeing himself in Trueblood. And this blindness allows him to experience vicariously the sin of incest in scintillating detail by getting Trueblood to recount vividly the terrible cold night when he made love to his daughter as his wife slept beside them. If Norton consciously saw anything of himself in Trueblood, he would fall outside the framework of white supremacy and black inferiority, and he would no longer be a great white redeemer. He would simply be a lecherous old man little different from the "nigger" whose taboo-breaking intrigues him. This sort of racial equality, grounded in common humanity, is precisely what Bledsoe cannot abide. His appeal is to the vanity and largesse of white supremacy. Racial equality—the idea that people are the same under the skin—is Bledsoe's private terror.

So he kicks the invisible man out of his college for putting Norton's white blindness at risk, for situating Norton precariously close to an experience of human commonality with an ignorant black sharecropper and, thus, close to an experience of something like both human vision and racial equality. Bledsoe—like such contemporary black leaders as Jesse Jackson, Al Sharpton, Julian *appear weak as to continue to gain the sympathy*

Bond, and the entire civil rights establishment—essentially sells a "Sambo" image of his own people, an image of black weakness and inferiority offered in *trade* to blind whites looking to buy an easy moral authority.

This points to a sad irony at the core of black-white relations in America. The price blacks pay for the mere illusion of recompense for past injustice *always* requires them—literally as well as metaphorically—to be "Sambo-ized," to be merchandised to whites as inferiors and victims. The Sambo doll, as an image of grotesque black inferiority sold to whites in homage to their superiority, is an ominous and recurring image in *Invisible Man*, a novel set in the era of segregation. Yet, even today, when people argue for diversity and, thus, for racial preferences, black students are effectively Sambo-ized. They are assigned an inferiority so intractable that nothing overcomes it, not even good schools and high family incomes.

When you give a racial preference to the child of two black professionals with advanced degrees and six-figure incomes—as entrée to a university that has not discriminated against blacks in more than sixty years—then you are clearly implying an inherent and irremediable black inferiority. You are saying that even the absence of racism and the fruits of a privileged life do not make it possible for blacks to compete with whites and Asians who may come from fractured homes and underprivileged backgrounds. So even the most gifted and affluent blacks—many of whom *can* compete on their own—must pull on the Sambo mask and reinvent themselves as the sort of inferiors that will trade well with white guilt. Even as opportunity virtually stalks their lives, they must learn to "lie to the white man."

21

THE RAGE OF INVISIBILITY

I always come away from arguments like the one with the "architect" of the Great Society feeling empty and frustrated. But these are only the polite feelings. Beneath them is always a palpable anger, potentially more intense even than any I felt back in the sixties when confronted by open racists. It is a sharp, bristling, and ego-fueled anger that, on the level of metaphor, would annihilate the offending party. It is triggered by encountering someone who cannot see you, even as he stands before you, because of all the presumptions he has made about you. Such a person has metaphorically annihilated you. He doesn't hit you; he simply doesn't see you, out of a conviction that there is nothing of you worth seeing beyond his own thin preconception of you. So you cease to exist in your own right and exist, instead, as a figment of his imagination. And this, of course, burns you up. You want to return fire, to employ a terrible violence—something, again on the metaphorical level, with the intimacy of, say, a switchblade or a tiny pistol. "Now you see me, don't you," you hiss into his ear as the blade goes in or the pistol pops.

This sort of rage is the human ego defending itself, and, thankfully, it very rarely plays out on the literal level because we are so conditioned to fear and suppress it. Also, as we age and the brickbats of life batter the ego down to size, as they say, there is less ego territory to defend, and in any case, there is less energy to waste on such defense. That said, this kind of anger is archetypal. It is always at work in the world.

People who are in the grip of white blindness, and thus unaware of their true motivations, always miss the human being inside the black skin, and so provoke this kind of anger. Your color represents you in the mind of such people. They will have built a large part of their moral identity and, possibly, their politics around how they respond to your color. Thus, a part of them— the moral part—is invested not in you but in some idea of what your color means. And when they see you—the individual— they instantly call to mind this investment and determine, once again, to honor it. They are very likely proud of the way they have learned to relate to your color, proud of the moral magnanimity it gives them an opportunity to express. So, in meeting you, they actually meet only a well-rehearsed and "better" part of themselves. Of course, if they are unapologetically racist, they would meet a well-rehearsed "superior" part of themselves. In either case, rage is likely to be your response.

Invisible Man opens with an extraordinary image of this rage. The invisible man is bumped by a white man on a dark street one night, and the man—"a tall blond"—calls him an insulting name. The invisible man grabs the white man by the lapels and demands that he apologize. He refuses, and the invisible man pulls the man's chin "down sharp upon the crown of my head, butting him as I had seen West Indians do, and I felt his flesh tear and blood gush out." The man still refuses to apologize, and the invisible man butts him again, and again, until he finally goes down. And once the white man is on the ground, the invisible man kicks him "repeatedly," yet the man continues to utter insults, though his mouth is now "frothy with blood." Finally, when the man is utterly helpless, the invisible man pulls out his knife, opens it with his teeth, and prepares to slit the man's throat. But at that instant, with the knife "slicing the air," the invisible man has an epiphany: "it occurred to me that the man had not *seen* me." Wow

This is the point at which the invisible man begins to understand that he is invisible and that the man, a white everyman, is blind. Instantly—and luckily for the white man—he is overcome by the irony that blindness and invisibility impose on the situation. "Something in this man's thick head had sprung out and beaten him within an inch of his life." In the man's head there was a "phantom," the idea of a nigger, an inferior being whom a white could insult at will and without consequence. This "phantom," rather than the individual human being he had bumped into, was all the white man could ever see; and so this phantom of his own making, this nigger, is what had leaped out of the darkness and beaten him nearly to death. The invisible man laughs at the irony of his "crazy discovery."

Yet, despite its great drama, I have never found this scene entirely convincing. We are asked to believe that the invisible man's sudden insight into blindness and invisibility, his almost literary comprehension of the moment's irony, is sufficient not only to dispel his anger but also to enable him to feel "sincere compassion" for this "poor blind fool." But can a murderous rage really be swept away by cool insight? Ellison's themes of invisibility and blindness would have stood even if he had allowed his young protagonist to kill the white man. But then the invisible man would have been a different sort of protagonist, one capable of rageful murder like Richard Wright's hero, Cross Damon, in *The Outsider*. *Invisible Man* required a more naive, even innocent, hero-narrator, so Ellison could not allow that knife to find its mark. Then, too, in 1953 when the novel was published, there would have been the practical matter of allowing a young black hero to kill a white man on the second page of the novel. So Ellison, unconvincingly, allows insight—epiphany—to still his hero's rage and save the "blind fool's" life.

And it is even more unconvincing because the rage the invisible man feels and the violence he acts out on the white man are quite convincing responses to white blindness. The invisible man's demand for an apology after the white man's first insult is effectively a demand to be seen and treated as a human being. It is born of his desire to be *visible*, a simple enough human desire. But the white man makes it clear that he would rather die than see the invisible man as a human being. Intractably committed to his blindness, this white man becomes a grinning tar baby— the more you hit him with hands and feet, the more you become stuck to him. Worse, each blow you deliver only infuriates *you* more until your own mounting anger finally spirals you into self-destruction. In the end your hands and feet are stuck to him, and he possesses you, all the while grinning impassively.

Tar babies infuriate and inflame the rages of pride by refusing to see the people who approach them. They assault with invisibility, and you want to annihilate them simply to be seen— perhaps the deepest human longing. But you only end up stuck to them. So Ellison chose the perfect conceit to reveal the effect of white blindness on its victims. Blithely, like an impervious tar baby, white blindness annihilates blacks with invisibility and so dupes us into a rageful pursuit of visibility. But after the rage and even violence, we are left to simmer in futility.

Well, this was the kind and quality of rage that I felt after my encounter with the "architect" of the Great Society. By now I have learned to sidestep such rage fairly well, to walk away from the tar baby, as it were. And today, in our age of white guilt, people or institutions in the grip of white blindness truly are tar babies. In the age of racism, white blindness was rooted in hate. Whites did not see you because their own identity—whiteness itself—was literally defined by your being less than human. But as infuriating as this kind of white blindness was, blacks could at least sneer back.

One of the few advantages of belonging to a despised group is that you so clearly owe nothing to your oppressor. In hatred and open oppression you are left, oddly, to possess yourself; behind the invisibility that hatred imposes there is what Ellison called a "margin of freedom" in which the oppressed *autonomously* reinvent themselves, making their own meaning and even culture. In the space of this freedom the oppressed will have their own mores and measures of character; their own ways of worship, rituals of romance, and music; and especially their own self-mocking absurdist humor. They will know that they are surviving against far greater odds than others, and despite the obvious unfairness of this, they will compose a brotherhood of the strong and assign themselves a broader and deeper humanity than others. Paradoxically, oppression always conveys a sense of superiority along with its abuses. This is why it is so profoundly mistaken to assume that racism and oppression automatically cause low self-esteem in blacks. The opposite is more likely the case.

In the age of racism blacks were not confused by white blindness, precisely because it was so openly antagonistic to us. When the invisible man is insulted by the white man, he does not wonder if the man is a friend or an enemy. He may worry about getting caught beating up a white man, but he has no doubt that he *should* beat him up. Racism forced an outward conformity and obeisance from blacks but not an internal agreement.

However, in the age of white guilt, white blindness has been driven not by racism but by the white need to *dissociate* from racism. Whites are blind to blacks as human beings today not out of bigotry but out of their obsession with achieving the dissociation they need to restore their moral authority. And when they find a way to dissociate from racism—"diversity," politically correct language, political liberalism itself—there is little incentive to understand blacks as *human beings*. Dissociation makes *whites* human again.

The white blindness that drives me to rage is, therefore, driven by the rage whites feel at having their humanity made invisible by the racist stigma. So it is not that whites want to be blind to the human circumstances and needs of blacks; rather, it is that they are fighting for their human visibility against a stigma, and in the process they become blind to all needs but their own.

The irony is that the "architect" felt rage toward me for precisely the same reason that I felt it toward him. We both felt assaulted by invisibility, and we both seethed at the other's impassive refusal to see past our race's reputation and into our individual humanity. We were each the other's tar baby. He was enraged with me because I was leaving him to languish in invisibility behind the racist stigma as if he were no better than the common run of whites, white Americans who had never lifted a finger to repair all the injustices done to blacks. His rage was that I would not *see* the goodness in his individual human heart. And he stood before me as the invisible man stood before his tormentor, trying to bully me into an acknowledgment of his humanity.

But I knew that he had simply made theater of his good intentions, hoping that money thrown at blameless poverty would win moral authority. That he was right in this, that he could win moral authority without ever seeing blacks as human beings like himself, is what tripped my rage. Effectively, he wanted me to give him credit for saving whites at the expense of blacks. So there we were, two Americans, a black and a white, caught in a kind of pas de deux of rage because we both perceived the other as blind to our humanity.

But I don't believe there was a genuine equivalency between us. I *saw* his humanity. I *saw* that he had behaved like most human beings when they are at first stigmatized. He had looked for the quickest and easiest way to live again without stigma. And, in his desperation, he had forgotten that blacks are human beings. It was precisely because I saw him as human that I understood the source of his blindness. And by continuing to see him as a human being, I could also understand his rage. My rage was that, forty-some years after the 1964 Civil Rights Act, he was utterly incapable of seeing the source of mine.

22

ELITISM AS VIRTUE

After the Supreme Court came down with its decision in the University of Michigan affirmative-action case, the *New York Times* columnist Maureen Dowd responded with one of the most vile columns I have ever seen in print. It was a screed, a public tantrum, a display of apoplectic and racist anger directed at Justice Clarence Thomas, who had written a powerful dissenting opinion in the case. But the invisibility rage that was so clearly behind Dowd's anger did not begin with her. It began in the flood of legal briefs submitted to the Court from over one hundred American institutions demanding that race preferences be kept alive. In other words, it began in white blindness, in that almost grim determination in whites to win dissociation from racism at virtually any cost. These institutions were fighting for their own visibility as fair and legitimate institutions open to all people. And Justice O'Connor's decision, built on the logic of all their briefs, is certainly one of the most unequivocal examples of white blindness ever written, more so—given

America's moral evolution since the nineteenth century—even than *Plessy v. Ferguson*. Without the slightest self-awareness, and writing largely in reference to unexamined social science clichés, O'Connor jerry-rigged a majority decision that had no real purpose beyond enabling America's institutions to dissociate themselves from racism. So here was a white justice, like my "architect," rather self-satisfied as she validated a policy *in the name of blacks* that served primarily white institutions.

But then Justice O'Connor was, herself, fighting for her visibility and moral authority against the racist stigma—a stigma that threatened to "annihilate" her legitimacy as a decent human being, not to mention as a sage Supreme Court justice. Especially as the Court's first woman she was under terrible, if unspoken, pressure not to be the justice who ended affirmative action. These are the pressures, I believe, that redirected her vision away from legitimate questions of racial discrimination and the law and toward the utterly artificial matter of diversity. "Diversity" is no more than code for white dissociation, and once O'Connor was in its thrall, she rendered herself utterly blind both to blacks as human beings and to the question of whether racial preferences were constitutional. And blind in this way, she wrote a decision that both assaulted and insulted black Americans with human invisibility.

Is it any wonder, then, that Justice Thomas's dissent in this same case is, above all else, a fiery and indignant demand that blacks be seen and understood first of all as human beings? Rare in Justice Thomas's legal writing, this dissent offers the human details of his own experience in the Ivy League and elsewhere. Just as O'Connor's decision was driven by a terror of human invisibility (being seen as a racist), Thomas's dissent was likewise driven by the same terror (being seen as no more than a black). Here is a colleague, someone ostensibly of his same philosophical orientation, who allows herself to be terrorized into a blindness toward black humanity, and thus toward *his* humanity. Worse, implied in her decision is a view of blacks as inferiors who simply cannot compete without *twenty-five* more years of white paternalism. Add to this her rather imperial tone and you have a perfect tar baby.

So just beneath the surface of Thomas's dissent there are echoes of the invisible man's rage, a rage that first of all wants visibility, wants the human effects of preferences on blacks to be seen and, failing that, wants to "annihilate" the enemy—not to murder but to annihilate the offending ideas that enthrall the enemy. In this case, the enemy is not only Justice O'Connor but also the archetypal white liberal, that blind, blithe, and infuriating figure whose social morality is nothing more than dissociation. In the end Thomas's dissent does "annihilate" these white liberals—and the entire canon of ideas that define them—by giving them no credit whatsoever for being on the side of good.

And then, with near-perfect predictability, Justice Thomas's scathing rejection of racial preferences sends Maureen Dowd—here standing in for white liberals everywhere—into an invisibility rage of her own. Clearly she feels metaphorically annihilated by the Thomas dissent, by his utter refusal to give liberals even the slightest moral credit for their support of preferences. He simply will not *see* people like Dowd as socially moral human beings just because they are aligned with "diversity"; thus, he effectively assaults them with invisibility. Here was a black man—and therefore someone with far greater moral authority on racial matters than the white Dowd—making it clear that her support for diversity made her at best a blind fool and at worst a moral fraud.

And this while she likely felt that her position on these policies brought her not only moral esteem but even a certain social and cultural superiority. After all, diversity is a "progressive" idea conceived of by an elite. It did not spring naturally from the American soil, as it were. And to embrace it is, at the very least, to have pretensions toward that elite. So possibly she drew yet more esteem because she supported diversity as a progressive sophistication, a difficult but civilizing idea that would have to be imposed from above on the common run of white Americans, who, after all, didn't even like affirmative action. In this age of white guilt, when dissociation from racism is the first pillar of decency, Dowd's alignment with diversity would have given her, if not a moral complacency, then at least a sense of moral legitimacy and confidence.

And then, in the face of her considerable self-esteem, comes the scathing dissent of Justice Thomas, which implies that, apart from what she might think of herself, she is incapable of seeing blacks as human beings and individuals and fellow citizens. She is incapable of considering the human effects—the stigmatization, the loss of incentives, and the encouragement of a victim-focused group identity—that preferences have on blacks. Between the lines in Thomas's dissent, people like Dowd are seen to make the classic liberal mistake of trying to pass off mere dissociation from racism as selfless virtue and real human empathy. Still, Dowd no doubt feels that diversity is real and that

Right. We don't have to do shit to help them, treat them with human dignity and address them or treat them any differently

whatever dissociates her from racism only reflects her expansive and modern humanity.

So Thomas's dissent effectively annihilates Maureen Dowd's conception of herself as a moral and socially responsible person. And this invisibility is simply too much to bear. Suddenly she is in a rage. In her column devoted to excoriating Thomas, she blurts out a word that chills the souls of all blacks. She says that instead of complaining, Clarence Thomas should show "gratitude" for affirmative action. Here, of course, she is trying to "annihilate" him, to put him in his place as an inferior who can advance only through the largesse of superiors like herself. Maureen Dowd, thinking herself quite incapable of racism, effectively calls Justice Thomas a nigger who—given his fundamental inferiority—should show "gratitude" to his white betters. In her rage, this ever so hip baby-boomer liberal invokes white supremacy itself to annihilate Thomas—in reaction to her sense of being annihilated by him. So mired in white blindness, so lost in the liberal orthodoxy that counts mere dissociation from racism as virtue, and so addicted to the easy moral esteem that comes to her from dissociation, Dowd plays the oldest race cards of all—I'm white and you're black, so shut up and be grateful for my magnanimity. It is as though in fighting for her human visibility she is really fighting for her superiority—a superiority that Thomas annihilated and that she now wants back.

Dowd illustrates the great internal contradiction of white liberalism: that its paternalism, its focus on whites rather than on blacks as the agents of change, allows white supremacy to slip in the back door and once again define the fundamental relationship between whites and blacks. So the very structure of the liberal faith—that whites and "society" must facilitate black uplift— locks white liberals into an unexamined white supremacy. They can't really believe in blacks but they *must* believe in whites. Whites are agents; blacks are agented.

So postsixties American liberalism preserves the old racist hierarchy of whites over blacks as virtue itself; and it grants all whites who identify with it a *new* superiority. In effect, it says you are morally superior to other whites and intellectually superior to blacks. The white liberal's reward is this feeling that because he is heir to the knowledge of the West, yet morally enlightened beyond the West's former bigotry, he is really a "new man," a better man than the world has seen before.

Post sixties American liberalism, are morally *think they* superior to other whites and intellectually superior to blacks.

HA HA HA

23

"THE NEW MAN"

This "new man" is essentially the liberal identity that came out of the great acknowledgment of the sixties. Social and political movements that want to redeem a country in some way often generate the idea of a "new man" who broadly embodies the movement's aspirations for the society. In many communist movements there was an ideal "comrade" whose character embodied the selflessness and common struggle that communism aspired to. Nationalist movements across the Third World have had "new men" who stood in sharp contrast to the subjugated colonial past by embracing not only independence but also the uniqueness of the national culture. Certainly the most diabolical "new man" of the twentieth century was Hitler's Aryan man, whose blue eyes, blond hair, and erect bearing embodied the supremacy of the Aryan race—a myth that hoped to redeem Germany's shame after its defeat in World War I. But the American liberal "new man" that emerged in the sixties also hoped to redeem through supremacy. He was superior to all previous Americans because he was without the great American shames of racism, sexism, militarism, and materialism.

But liberalism back in the age of racism had not produced a "new man." This was classic Jeffersonian liberalism, grounded in timeless democratic principles and a commitment to individual freedom. Its argument was only that America had betrayed its great principles. And the civil rights victory of the mid-sixties was seen as a victory of principles rather than of a "new man" who embodied the nation's redemption.

But, then, the white guilt that followed gave America an entirely new political and cultural liberalism—a liberalism of *dissociation.* In the age of white guilt the American struggle was no longer over betrayed principles; rather, it was a struggle for moral authority. So by the late sixties American liberalism had begun to shift from its time-honored focus on principles and individual freedom to a new focus on dissociation. Suddenly there was a need for a "new man," or more accurately a "dissociated man," someone so conspicuously cleansed of racism, sexism, and militarism that he would be a carrier of moral authority and legitimacy.

You could already see this liberal "new man" on campuses in the late sixties among both faculty and students. And even then you could sense that he had fallen into a kind of trap. Dissociation is inherently elitist. Automatically, it creates a new kind of American, one who is *better* than most Americans because he has conspicuously dissociated from the litany of American sins. Thus, elitism, in itself, became a form of dissociation, a way to become a "new man," to show oneself better than most Americans and, thus, worthy of moral authority. And, of course, one *wanted* to be better than most Americans had been in racial matters. One wanted a moral elitism in relation to the nation's bigotries and bigots. But over time, as elitism became more entrenched as dissociation, a new American archetype emerged: the unreconstructed white American, the white who has failed to dissociate from the country's racist past. Such whites may or may not actually be racist, but their failure to dissociate in this age of white guilt means they carry no moral authority, and add nothing to the legitimacy of the institutions they are a part of.

This is how postsixties liberalism—grounded in dissociation and therefore elitism—has divided the country. And since the sixties, these divisions have only deepened, giving us today a nation divided into so-called red and blue states. Blue states are more dissociational and elitist; red states tend to prefer a liberalism of principle more than dissociation. But it was white guilt, this yawning vacuum of authority, that set the forces in play that would leave us divided.

Because dissociation is a *claim* of superiority, it generates a kind of collective narcissism—an irrational yet utterly certain belief in the moral superiority of postsixties, dissociational liberalism. In this liberalism one does not argue by logic or principle; ones argues by dissociation. Only in dissociation are authority, legitimacy, and power available. This grounding in dissociation, with its assertion of moral superiority, is what gives today's liberalism its narcissistic quality.

And then a perfect coming together: a white, middle-class, baby-boomer generation—already rather inflated by postwar prosperity and high parental expectations—with a political and cultural liberalism that grants moral superiority on top of everything else.

This, I sense, has much to do with the narcissistic inflation that was so obvious in Maureen Dowd as she railed away at Justice Thomas. She came from that generation whose parents were tainted (stigmatized) by their link to America's racist and militaristic past—people who likely supported the military intervention in Vietnam, and who preferred blacks to "go slow" in their push for freedom. Such parents could be easily condescended to (as unreconstructed whites) by their children, who saw themselves as smarter, more sophisticated, and certainly more aligned with moral truth. The liberalism that boomers like Dowd embraced finished off a sense of generational superiority. Now, added to the blessings of prosperity and opportunity, was an easy road to moral character as well: dissociation.

What was so striking about Dowd's invisibility rage was that it also seemed to be narcissistic rage. Affirmative action exists solely for the purpose of white dissociation. And when Justice Thomas attacked it, he cut to the heart of Dowd's moral vanity. He made it clear that she was not a "new man," that her elitist conception of herself as someone of greater moral sensibility than unreconstructed whites was a delusion. By implication, he attacked dissociation itself as a false morality. This was annihilation of the most complete kind because it took from her a kind of beauty—a look of moral superiority that served her in the world like a pretty face.

So there was woundedness in her rage. And in her hurt, she became a "redneck," an unreconstructed white. She made Thomas into an inferior who owed her "gratitude."

In the 2004 presidential election John Kerry ran as the "new man" candidate against an unreconstructed George Bush. As with Dowd and Thomas, here was a classic battle between the elitist culture of dissociation and the unreconstructed culture of principle and traditional values. Kerry was the elitist liberal, like Dowd, all the way down to a personal narcissism—two-hundred-dollar haircuts, rumors of Botox. He would fight the same war as Bush, but he would fight a "more sensitive" war. In other words, he had mastered the craft of dissociation. He would bring Europe on board, respect the UN. He would *dissociate* America from its image as an imperialistic power.

Kerry seemed completely defined as a candidate by the mechanisms of white guilt. Even invisibility rage was exploited to win votes. "Bush hating"—a kind of collective invisibility rage—had much to do with the refusal of this unreconstructed white man from Texas to see and honor the elitism of the left. Bush infuriated the left not because his positions were vastly different from theirs—both candidates supported the war—but because he seemed unreconstructed by dissociation and therefore blind to the higher humanity they had achieved through dissociation. Even though Kerry also supported the war, he hoped his dissociation from America's imperialist image would win him the following of Bush haters who were clearly against the war.

But Kerry's loss to Bush makes an important point. Unreconstructed whites in America are not so unreconstructed anymore. Racism and imperial ambition no longer characterize the attitudes of most Americans. So there is less and less desperation in the society for the palliative of dissociation. Whatever most Americans may think about President Bush and his policies, they simply do not believe that he is a racist and an imperialist. The larger public, unlike the nation's institutions and its liberal elite, feels less and less need for dissociation.

24

SELF-DESTRUCTION

For some time now the American political culture has labeled people like myself "black conservatives." I remember well how shocked and resentful I was when I first began to hear myself spoken of in this way. And I remember fierce arguments, outraged denials. Who wants to be reduced to a label? Then, slowly, I began to realize that resistance was futile, that something much bigger than I was at work. The political culture had somehow, out of some special squeeze of forces, created a new, if minor, archetype—the black conservative—and my fate had been sealed before I knew it. It was as if a totalitarian government had given me a tiny house to live in and said I would have to live in it the rest of my life. Not much to do but move in and try to make myself comfortable.

But what were the forces that created this archetype? Certainly there had always been black Republicans, and many of the values that we refer to today as conservative were quite prominent in the black community I grew up in. On social issues blacks tend to poll more conservatively than whites. One poll even had 88 percent of blacks opposing racial preferences. So why this new prejudice that when "black conservative" is not an oxymoron it is a novelty?

I think the answer begins in the idea that has defined American liberalism since the sixties: that dissociation is virtue. Because this liberalism was a response to white guilt, dissociation from racism and other American shames was always its overriding obsession. The liberal "new man" embraced dissociation as the virtue that brought legitimacy to his other virtues. After all, what would it matter that he had integrity in business if he was a racist? So, above all else, the liberal new man practiced dissociation. And it was such a new man—though actually a woman, a colleague—who inadvertently gave me a first glimpse of this new archetype, the black conservative.

One day back in the early eighties I sat in a curriculum meeting listening as a colleague—I will call her Betty—pitched a proposal for a new course in "ethnic literature." In those days English departments like mine were still vaguely divided between the "graybeards" and the baby boomers, the former being traditionalists—usually older white men—and the latter being junior faculty looking for a career path in race and gender studies, deconstructionism, the new historicism, postmodernism, and so on. Though I was a baby boomer by age, I identified more with the traditionalism of the graybeards. The new isms seemed nihilistic and a little fraudulent to me, and they attracted a rather slippery group of self-promoting and self-important spokesmen who seemed more dissemblers than real thinkers. And I was especially suspicious of any course outside the Anthropology

Department with the word "ethnic" in its title. What could it possibly mean? If it was simply literature by nonwhites, then why not say so? If it referred to culture, wouldn't French and English writers qualify? If not, why not? What unifying concepts were at work in the term "ethnic literature"? And who might be an ethnic writer? Philip Roth? V. S. Naipaul?

Of course I knew that Betty's proposal would sail right through that day. The alignment of power was already clearly in the boomers' favor and "ethnic" was a word to conjure with. This was so, I know now, because it was a *dissociational* word, a word that dissociated this writing and the professors who taught it from the presumed racism and bigotry of the great Western literary canon. It was a *dissociational* class that Betty was proposing, and so its appeal was not to literary excellence but to social virtue. Betty did not argue the excellence of the writers she wanted to include; she argued that our student body was "multicultural" and that "these students" deserved to see their cultural experience represented in literature. Here she moved beyond simple dissociation into protest. The class would challenge the hegemony of Western notions of literary excellence. And it would suggest that inclusion was effectively a literary value in its own right, even that race and ethnicity— if they referred to formerly oppressed people of color—also constituted a kind of literary merit.

This was more than Betty said, but not more than she meant. She was a new man. Dissociation was her great truth, and it caused her, finally, to dissociate from literary excellence itself as if from racism. After all, excellence was unforgivingly exclusionary. It cared nothing that minorities were underrepresented in the canon. So, like liberal new men across academe, Betty was pushed backward by her faith in dissociation into an embrace of mediocrity as a means to social fairness. For her, an openness to mediocrity served dissociation; therefore, it brought a moral authority that real excellence could never bring. And she was supported in this by all the new relativistic literary theory that dissembled literary excellence to the point that comic books became legitimate "texts" for study. She offered a list of writers she would assign in the class, but Nikki Giovanni and Maxine Hong Kingston were the only names I recognized.

But it was not until each member of the committee was asked to comment on her proposal that I glimpsed for the first time this new phenomenon, the black conservative. One by one each committee member spoke, and virtually all the comments were unctuously favorable. Betty was thanked for her "foresight," praised for "meeting this need." And there were the usual lamentations over how "alienated" our minority students were, and about how few of them ever became English majors. Then it was my turn to say something. I had been sitting there preparing to be the skunk at the picnic, to say frankly why I thought this was a bad idea. My belief was that minority writers should be included in our mainstream literature classes by merit. This would mean two things: that they would be respected for their talent rather than endured for their color and that they would be read by all our students on a regular basis. An ethnic literature class would only create a literary ghetto of mediocre writers, an "affirmative-action" class in which even great writers would be diminished. I would confess my own regret at having taught a course called "Afro-American Literature." The good fight, I wanted to say, was for mainstream respect and exposure. All this and more was on the tip of my tongue, but when my turn to speak came, Betty said, "I think we can all agree that it's not necessary to hear from Shelby. He'll be with me." She spoke as if doing the committee a kindness. My race so obviously signaled my support for her proposal that hearing from me would only waste the committee's time and my energy.

Talk about invisibility rage! I started to explode. My head filled with ugly, even brutal, epithets that I wanted to spit back at her. But instead I gave out a long sigh—"Oh, God"—and contained myself.

"So you think I'm an automatic vote for you because I'm black?"

Betty was no shrinking violet. She could muscle people, and somewhere inside her there was an unassuageable anger. She met my cold gaze without flinching.

"Well, doesn't being black make you an automatic on this?"

"I suppose you don't see anything racist in what you're saying?"

"No I don't. Come on, Shelby. Don't give me a hard time. How in God's name are you going be anything but in favor of an ethnic literature class?"

"Betty, I'm going to vote against your proposal every chance I get. But before I tell you why, I would like an apology." Now it was my turn to hold her gaze. We could all literally hear the silence in the room.

After many long seconds she said, "All right, I apologize if I took you for granted. But I don't see how a black man can be against a class like this. Half the writers will be black. You'll be voting against your own people."

And there it was, my first little glimpse of the new cultural archetype, the black conservative. Years would pass before the term "black conservative" gained common currency, but right there I could see that a new idea of social virtue was so solidly in place that it had already generated a despised devil figure to personify the evil it hoped to eliminate. Before this, a black conservative was simply a black person who was conservative. But this idea of social virtue made any black who opposed it *evil*, so that "black conservative" and "evil" became synonymous. What Betty could never understand was that I had no interest in a social virtue based on nothing more than white people dissociating from the nation's racial shame, though I could not have said it this way at the time. And this was the failing that made me a black conservative. Of course, there were crumbs that would fall to minorities for indulging whites in this way—things precisely like these ill-conceived ethnic literature classes and the weak-paying pickup jobs that minorities would get teaching them. But this is humiliating stuff, a shuffle and a bow for a tossed coin. Still, even back then, it was clear that the deal had already been struck. Easy dissociation for whites and crumbs for blacks would be the *normative* institutional idea of social virtue.

What makes one a black conservative is simply opposing this deal. It is a deal made of what is low and cowardly in both races.

Of course, Betty's proposed class sailed right through that committee over all my objections and straight into the curriculum, where some version of it no doubt remains today.

Moreover, today literature classes amorphously designed around ethnicity are ubiquitous in American universities. I don't know Betty anymore. Our relationship chilled after our little dustup. But my guess is that she is quite happy with this development.

But I suspect that something else was going on with Betty, something that points to a larger corruption. Betty herself did not have an advanced degree like most others in the department, and her poetry was thought unremarkable by many. She was not a particularly good teacher and she did not have tenure. It is not unreasonable to suspect that, on some level, her own mediocrity as a writer and teacher may have pushed her to choose dissociation as an avenue to success in the department over the more traditional path of creative achievement and teaching excellence. If she was not much of a poet or teacher, she would serve the greater good by bringing us the literature of victims, by correcting for the arrogance of the Western canon, and by making the point that "inclusion" was now a literary value in its own right.

In other words, Betty knew instinctively that in the age of white guilt there was a market in dissociation. Universities could no longer afford to devote themselves singularly to excellence. Now they also had to win dissociation. Dissociation had become an institutional imperative. So Betty could argue—with this imperative like a wind at her back—that we didn't need a new undergraduate seminar on Milton or Chaucer when there was no place in the curriculum for "ethnic" writers. In fact, the sacrifice of excellence *was* the display of social virtue that won dissociation.

*   *   *

Within my university, and virtually all others across the nation, dissociation became a rich vein of power. People like Betty could build careers by arguing social virtue *at the expense* of excellence. Excellence and merit became "oppressive" terms within the academy because they were deemed the special province of privileged whites—no more than the fruits of an exclusionary, hierarchical, and discriminatory society. They impeded rather than expedited dissociation, and thus they actually *associated* the institution with racism. So here, in this prejudicial attitude toward excellence—this feeling that merit no more than preserves white privilege—there was a clear *incentive* for mediocrity and a *disincentive* for excellence within America's system of higher education. If Betty's ethnic literature class inadvertently championed mediocrity and, worse, identified that mediocrity with minority writers, then this sacrifice of excellence, this stigmatization of minorities, only made for a more dramatic white dissociation from racism.

The silly implication of Betty's argument was that she was simply more anguished by racism than she was excited about exposing students to great literature. After all, universities had taught great literature for centuries and failed to prevent racism. Where was the moral authority of a literary excellence, she essentially argued, that had in no way prevented the plunder of the world's colored peoples? Hadn't Shakespeare preceded colonial empire? And hadn't certain indisputably excellent writers— Kipling, Conrad, Hemingway, Faulkner, and many others— been apologists for white supremacy? Didn't we cringe when the rare black character came shuffling onstage in their works, hat in hand, and giving life to the most prosaic stereotypes? Had literary genius spared these writers from white blindness in the form of common bigotry? So possibly an angry, if untalented, black writer was not so bad. And the mere racialism and protest in the later work of genuinely talented writers like James Baldwin and Toni Morrison was not so bad either. If these writers had allowed a misplaced group loyalty—and some mythical idea of "blackness"—to render them trite, their ubiquity on university reading lists showed a *white* openness to the pained "truth" of black anger.

I had not understood, at the time of my ruckus with Betty, how vast the vacuum of moral authority at the center of American life really was. Nor had I understood that when a society has a great need like this, when the very legitimacy of its institutions must constantly be proven, power *shifts* to those like Betty who claim to meet that need. White guilt had put a new power into play in American society, and had made a new class of people—the Bettys of the world—powerful. My argument for excellence and merit was supported by a waning power. Even then, in the early eighties, there was no longer enough authority to give excellence priority over things like "diversity" and "inclusion."

But dissociation is a power that *always* works by eroding the quality of its host institution. It is at war not only with excellence, but also with intellectual difficulty and accountability of any kind. In this age of white guilt, these things have been stigmatized as oppressive and unnecessarily fastidious. Dissociation is to make things easier. And there is no better example of the self-destruction that dissociation brings to institutions than the American public schools. Those who would take power by making things easier have all but destroyed what was once the greatest public education system in the world. In more liberal states like California, where dissociation has been an orthodoxy if not a religion, the schools are even worse than elsewhere.

And this is also the power that Betty used to stigmatize me as a black conservative—that is, someone you dissociate from to win moral authority.

PART FOUR

DISSOCIATION AND CULTURE

25

THE COUNTERCULTURE ESTABLISHMENT

The last mile of my slow trek back down Toro Canyon was done in the dark. I had misjudged how fast the winter sun drops, especially when one is walled in on two sides at the bottom of a canyon. At four o'clock I saw sunlight on the eastern face of the canyon, but already it was as cool as night down where I walked. By four-thirty it was dark. Still, the path was broad, and I knew it well. So I walked even slower, enjoying my little Chautauqua, stopping now and then to jot a note in the hazy dark.

When I finally reached the car, the Clinton-Lewinsky mess was still in high scream all over the radio. I quickly turned it off. For one thing, I thought I had at least the beginning of an answer to the dilemma I had set for myself that morning coming out of Los Angeles. Why had it now begun to look as though President Clinton might survive an ugly sex scandal that would surely have brought down President Eisenhower back in the fifties? And, conversely, why would President Eisenhower's saying "nigger" on the golf course have no effect on his presidency when it would almost certainly have ended the Clinton presidency? In one era giving in to lust was the unpardonable sin; in another, giving in to racism.

In Clinton's era white guilt was the great moral vacuum that had to be filled in order to hold the democracy together. Without the moral authority to fill this vacuum, the government itself, not to mention the other institutions in society, would be without legitimacy—a formula for revolution the world over. Today I am a citizen who honors his country because it responded—albeit very badly in the realm of public policy—to white guilt. It acknowledged its profound racial transgressions and determined to end them. Had America not done this, the government would have had no legitimacy for me, and I would most certainly have left my country or attacked it, as would any self-respecting person in that circumstance.

Multiracial societies, where prejudice has been allowed to create deep inequalities over time, require *moral* balancing. They cannot recover their authority and legitimacy without a self-conscious and explicit *social* morality.

And this was the social and historical imperative that gave moral context to President Clinton's little imbroglio. White guilt meant that America had long ago decided to make *social* morality more important than *individual* morality because there was simply no other way to preserve the Union. Of course, rather than a serious social morality focused on fairness and human development, we got the jerry-built virtue of dissociation. Nevertheless, it was history's elevation of social morality that diminished the importance of President Clinton's lapse in individual morality.

As America's first baby-boomer president, President Clinton was from the generation that invented the practice of using social morality as a *license* to disregard individual morality: "What counts is human equality and feeding the poor, not whom I sleep with." Clearly, the idea that social morality was the more important of the two moralities was one of the great justifications for the sexual revolution of the seventies: "Free sex is not evil; racism and war are evil." And, of course, President Clinton was defended in many quarters by the moral framework of the sexual revolution: that one's social morality should be judged by a puritanical standard, while only nonjudgment and relativism should apply to one's sexual practices.

The sexual revolution owes much to white guilt, since it is difficult to imagine how such a self-absorbed revolution could have thrived without the cover and justification provided by the new social morality that white guilt had made so important in the culture. It goes too far to suggest that white guilt *caused* the sexual revolution. But then again, it did make such a revolution virtually inevitable. It was white guilt that powerfully stigmatized (with racism, militarism, etc.) precisely the traditional values that had always prevented a sexual revolution. Also, in making social morality the nation's preeminent morality, white guilt gave people the means to feel virtuous even as they marched into the sexual revolution.

So President Clinton was lucky to make his mistake in the age of white guilt. And he was lucky again that this social morality, which made him virtuous despite his personal lapses, was nothing more than the virtue of dissociation—an ersatz virtue that he could achieve through mere identification. To be a "moral man" in the most important way he had only to *identify* himself with dissociation. He would "mend not end" affirmative action. He would make black church appearances a staple of his presidency. True to his generation, he would be cool toward the military. Even his litany of bad habits from infidelity to chronic lateness would identify him as "America's first black president." So here we had—through the magic of dissociation by mere identification—an entirely emblematic social virtuousness that was enough to preserve the president in office.

Had President Clinton used the word "nigger," he would have *associated* with white supremacy and militarism, with the excesses of empire. Moral authority would have been utterly impossible. Today the legitimacy of the American presidency is inextricably tied to an *explicit,* if only symbolic, dissociation from the nation's racist past. So President Clinton had the "virtue" that counted in his era, just as President Eisenhower had the traditional values, at least as far as appearances went, that counted in his.

26

A CULTURE WAR

When I finally left the Great Society programs I had worked in and returned to graduate school, I was not a likely candidate for the designation I seemed to have earned later in life: "black conservative." Despite all the corruption and incompetence I had seen in those programs—and despite my happiness in getting away to the comparative quiet of graduate school—I was still politically very far to the left. If I was not as intensely "black" (by then a term of political identity) as I had been in college, I nevertheless wore my blackness on my sleeve even as I read Proust and Kafka and Dostoyevsky.

I was infected with an odd form of schizophrenia that I have come to see in many black academics and professionals of my generation. I was happy to be back in school "taking care of business," and I enjoyed all that I was learning. But there was also an expectation on campus that I "be black" in interesting and politicized ways. As a black you were a bit of an exhibit on these largely white campuses. And one way I carried this burden—

without thinking much about it—was to be both "black" and far left. If I was hazy about what either of these things actually meant, I did know the postures, the right-on phrases, and the stereotyped ideas that fit me easily into the community. It never occurred to me—as it doesn't occur to many young blacks today—that a person of my race and background could be conservative without betraying himself profoundly. So I went on laboring my way through graduate school like a perfectly respectable petit bourgeois, yet thinking myself—on the rare occasions when I took stock—the exponent of a radical politics of alienation.

I often wonder these days what might have happened to my generation of black academics and intellectuals if, back then, we had built a politics based on the way we actually lived. Eventually, I did precisely this for one reason: I got very tired of the schizophrenia. Elsewhere I have called this "race fatigue," an almost existential weariness with things racial, not because you don't care, but because the racial identity you are pressured to squeeze into is a mask you wear only out of calculation. This mask is untethered from your real life so that, over time, it draws you into a corrupting falseness—and an inner duplicity—that grows more and more rigid with the years. Ultimately it affects the integrity of your personality. You have to start living off rationalizations and falsehoods that a part of you *knows* to be false.

This schizophrenia was everywhere evident among blacks when the comedian Bill Cosby famously criticized poor blacks for not taking more responsibility for themselves and their children. Black elites who would never utter such a statement— for fear of seeming to betray their identity—*knew* that Cosby was absolutely right. A 70 percent illegitimacy rate among all blacks (90 percent in certain inner cities) pretty much makes the point that there is a responsibility problem. To know this, as all blacks do, and to have to pretend that it is not strictly true or that certain "systemic" forces are more responsible than blacks themselves is knowingly to lie to oneself. You sensed in the umbrage and anger in Cosby's voice when he made these statements that he had finally just had it, that race fatigue had overwhelmed him, that he was tired of living a lie. "You're asking me to lie in order to be black," he seemed to say, "and I won't do it anymore." Predictably, many blacks—quite accustomed to squeezing themselves into a mask of blackness and living schizophrenically—chastised Cosby or quibbled with his choice of words or his tone of voice.

Where did this pressure to live schizophrenically come from?

For me it began in the culture war that developed after the sixties. People like the above-mentioned Betty assumed that my skin color automatically put me on the left side of hostilities in this war. And this might not have bothered me if the left I was assumed a part of had still been like the left I had grown up in. But this was no longer the left that banked black freedom on democratic principles and black advancement on individual responsibility. It did not exclaim, as was the mantra of the early civil rights worker, "I am a man." The emphasis then had been on the fundamental humanity and individuality of blacks, and on the illegitimacy of any government's attempt to make us *be a race*. The left back then did not take race seriously; it wanted to puncture the illusion of race so that we could live as free individuals. (It fought *against* having to identify one's race on job and school applications, as did the "conservative" Ward Connerly in a recent California ballot initiative.) But the left that Betty assumed I belonged to was not this old left of individual freedom, principles, and responsibilities; it was a left that turned against all these things. It was a left of dissociation.

When the American left responded to the crisis of white guilt, and began to define social virtue as mere dissociation, it effectively started the culture war. Dissociation is *always* achieved at the expense of democratic principles and demanding values grounded in fairness and individual responsibility—what in shorthand might be called "the culture of principle." Dissociation wants to "engineer," "defer," and "relativize" *around* precisely this culture of principle in order to expediently garner moral authority and legitimacy. So there it was, beginning in the sixties, a culture war between two political and moral cultures, one grounded in principle and values, the other in dissociation—the former broadly focusing the right, the latter focusing the left.

By the mid-eighties the schizophrenia imposed on me as a black who was identified with the left had become unbearable. I had no interest in becoming a conservative. I just instinctively disliked the left's disregard of principles that had *always* been important to me. Worse, I had become terrified of the Faustian bargain waiting for me at the doorway to the left: we'll throw you a bone like affirmative action if you'll just let us reduce you to your race so we can take moral authority for "helping" you. When they called you a nigger back in the days of segregation, at least they didn't ask you to be grateful. So by the mid-eighties I was asked by the left to believe in dissociation rather than in demanding principles as the road to black advancement. Or, if I chose to continue believing in principles, I was asked to lie about it and say that continuing racism justified sparing blacks the rigors of principle.

Around this time I began to have many little "Cosby moments," as we might call them today. In meetings, at faculty parties or dinners, or simply in innocent encounters on campus, someone would make a dissociational comment as if uttering a self-evident truth—"What does merit mean, anyway?"; "We must improve the climate here for women and minorities"; "The minority voices in my classes are so important"—and then I would erupt. Such banalities spoke of an entire Orwellian culture composed of glassy-eyed true believers and cunning power-mongers like Betty. The schizophrenia I carried to survive in that culture made me more and more alienated and angry. Every relationship I had began to suffer, and by the late eighties, every single one of them had ended. I would run into people who had been closer than family, people who had known my children in infancy, and there would be deep awkwardness, a chilling smile. And certainly my heart, too, had gone cold. The culture war had made me fight too hard for my individuality, and I became a little merciless, happy to reject before I was rejected.

At the heart of this culture war there remains a terrible contra-diction: the new "progressiveness" that America achieved around race after the sixties was accompanied by considerable cultural decline. The problem is that the dissociational left destroys the principles that would realize its goals, and the right lacks the moral authority to enforce those selfsame principles. The result is a kind of impotence. Whether the problem is school reform or minority poverty, there has been no way to bring demanding principles to bear. So, as Americans have made great moral progress where the nation's old sins are concerned, they have also stood by helplessly as the nation's public schools have declined right before their eyes, and as inner-city poverty has become more intractable and isolating than ever. (Inner-city black English diverges more from standard English today than it did in the fifties.) The nation's moral development has correlated to a deepening powerlessness in the face of its social problems—this the legacy of a white guilt–inspired culture war that allows social problems to be addressed only by dissociation.

This contradiction has also more and more shaped America's political landscape. The left abandoned its compassionate Jeffersonian liberalism of the early civil rights era in favor of the dissociation that enabled it to respond to the crisis of white guilt (broadened by the sins of sexism, Vietnam, and environmental indifference). In this crisis, if you could win moral authority for a society threatened with revolution, you would be given real political power. So, in trading in principles for dissociation, the left stumbled onto the formula for power that would see it through the next several decades.

But this was a deal with the devil. In choosing dissociation over principles the left became impotent; without demanding principles it could not solve the very social problems that justified its existence. Principles *associated;* they didn't dissociate. Therefore, even as the left garnered great moral authority for being socially concerned, it stood handcuffed as a black underclass burgeoned forth in America's inner cities, and it looked on helplessly as the greatest public school system in the world collapsed into one of the worst in the world. In the end, the devil got the better part of his bargain with the left. Today's left is both impotent before social problems and alienated from the principles that might solve those problems.

What about the right?

The right today enjoys a new political and cultural ascendancy for two reasons. First, the left has effectively ceded its old territory—compassionate Jeffersonian liberalism—to the right, thereby ceding to it precisely the democratic principles and values of individual freedom and responsibility that have made America a great nation despite its many betrayals of these principles. The second reason is that today's right has been chastened and now understands that racism, sexism, and reckless militarism are *morally* wrong.

The right of my segregated childhood took white supremacy to be the natural order of the world and sought to preserve it. The conservatism of that era was not simply about free markets and smaller government. It also wanted to "conserve" the prevailing racial hierarchy that made America a "white man's country." This history *associated* conservatism with the nation's evils. And today all forms and schools of conservatism remain stigmatized as carriers of these evils.

In fact, most of today's conservatives sound like Martin Luther King in 1963. Contemporary conservatism treats race with precisely the same compassionate Jefferson liberalism that Martin Luther King articulated in his "I Have a Dream" speech. Is there, on the right, a covert, unspoken loyalty to racial hierarchy, a quiet atavistic commitment to white supremacy? In the hearts of some there must be. There are fools and devils everywhere. But today's right has made itself *accountable* to the democratic and *moral* vision of the early Martin Luther King.

In many ways, the special character of contemporary conservatism comes from the fact that it is a *reaction* to the cultural decline caused by the culture of dissociation. This conservatism tends to think of itself as a historical corrective. Its great mission is to reassert principle *as reform*. For decades now it has been preoccupied with social problems that were once the sole province of the left—education reform, inner-city poverty, marriage and family issues, youth culture, and so on.

And yet, white guilt means that this reformist conservatism still labors under a stigma. It struggles against an opposition that now operates more by association and dissociation than by reason and principle. A great power for today's left is the power of association. Whether the issue is Social Security, school reform, or even war, the left forces the right to do battle with associations drawn from an imagery of America's past evils. The Iraq war is the rebirth of American imperialism. Private retirement accounts privilege the rich. Accountability in school reform blames the victims of underfunded schools. Reasoning against an association is like punching a shadow.

Clearly a mission of the current Bush presidency has been to destigmatize contemporary conservatism. Here Bush has accepted that he operates in the age of white guilt, and—with good and bad results—he has brought dissociation to conservatism. He appoints minorities at every opportunity and to the highest levels of government. His faith-based initiative directly addresses poverty through the institution of the black church. His "bigotry of low expectations" statement was the first and most far-reaching enunciation of American social policy since Lyndon Johnson's Howard University speech. It offered a new direction for social reform and, especially, a new theory: *dissociation from the racist past through principle and individual responsibility* rather than at the expense of these things. Bush is the first conservative president to openly compete with the left in the arena of ideas around poverty, education, and race. He has attempted to establish conservatism as a philosophy of *social* reform.

But in our deepening culture war, Bush has endured a remarkable degree of contempt from many of his opponents, more contempt than even the worst Bush caricatures would justify. One reason for this is that he sits atop a historical, cultural, and even political correction that is much larger than himself. And this correction—this historical pressure to correct for the many excesses of the age of white guilt—harshly *judges* people on the dissociational left. It tells them that they were wrong—one of the most unsettling things anyone can be told. It tells them that they failed the country out of a self-congratulating moral elitism— that they refused to enforce demanding principles or to ask for more responsibility from those they claimed to feel compassion for, and that they flattered themselves with a "progressivism" of mere moral relativism even as the culture declined all around them. What is more, there is an utter confidence at the center of this corrective. It has spawned an entire alternative media that scolds, belittles, and even scorns the dissociational left twenty-four hours a day. And whenever people feel shamed, there is a blowback.

Historical corrections always come cruelly. They shame as a means to power and transformation. This is how the baby-boomer dissociational left defeated its parents' generation. And this is how history is once again moving. Bush is only the current face of an ascending historical judgment.

When I departed from the left in the late eighties, it wasn't because I was prescient enough to see the historical correction that was already building. I simply couldn't take the schizophrenia required to stay in the cultural and political world that I had always belonged to. But as my father-in-law used to say, "You go to the dentist with a toothache and he pours hot tar on your head." I was caught in the defining contradiction of the culture war: on one side no enforcement of principle; on the other side the stigmatization that prevents enforcement. I escaped schizophrenia but I walked right into stigmatization as an Uncle Tom. I was happier living more consistently with myself, but it was suddenly extremely difficult to connect with other blacks and liberal whites. My only trick as a writer has been to write about America without the schizophrenia imposed on blacks by the culture war. I don't have to "protect" blacks or any other group by pretending that certain self-serving lies ("systemic" racism remains a barrier) are true. That kind of thing almost smothered my life as a free man. And if I've learned anything in all of this, it is that if you want to be free, you have to make yourself that way and pay whatever price the world exacts. So I am quite free now. And it is the rare black who gets to live without the world expecting him to pretend. So I don't mind so much that little bit of hot tar the world has poured on my head.

* * *

There is a point at which westbound Highway 68 merges with Highway 1, the old Pacific Coast Highway. When this happens you are already in town. Just before you, as if you were seeing it in a movie, the tree-muted lights of Monterey spill down a long slope of coastal mountain to meet the Monterey Bay. If this has always been a sweet sight for me, it was even sweeter on that night. Only a few hours later I started my little Chautauqua all over again, only this time on paper.

About the author

About the book

Read on

Insights,
Interviews
& More . . .

Shelby Steele
Literary Beginnings

Rita Steele

WHEN I WAS TWELVE YEARS OLD I was
transferred out of an all-black segregated
school and into an all-white school
nearby. For this simple transfer to occur
in the segregated Chicago of the late
fifties, my parents had to launch a mini
civil rights movement of their own.
There were many confrontations with
local authorities, and a boycott that closed
the all-black school for a full year. At the
center of this maelstrom my parents were
often distracted, sometimes terrorized,
and always eaten up with outrage. They

saw themselves misquoted in the newspapers, and everywhere heard lies about themselves. On certain occasions the phone would ring, a chill would infuse the house, and I would be sent away "just to play it safe."

Yet, somehow, all of this led to a very positive change in my life. After a year of living with frayed nerves I had begun to feel an unassuageable fatigue and irritability, as if I had gone from childhood immediately into old age. But toward the end of that year one of the most important events in my life took place: my new teacher at the white school I had transferred into gave me a book to read, *Kit Carson and the Pony Express.*

Of course, after six years of segregated education, I was virtually illiterate. Yet I accepted this thin volume—written at a sixth-grade level—as if I was going to rush home and finish it off in a single sitting. In fact, it took me almost nine months of steady effort to read this small book from beginning to end. No one helped me as I labored to unravel its hieroglyphics. But gradually I came to see and feel the relationship between these marks on paper—language—and life itself. When I finally finished the book, the written word and the heroic adventures of Kit Carson were one, and from then on I could no longer stand the thought of being without a book. On the day I finished *Kit Carson* I went to the local drug store and purchased *The Mud Hen* ▶

> 66 Toward the end of that year one of the most important events in my life took place: my new teacher at the white school I had transferred into gave me a book to read, *Kit Carson and the Pony Express.* 99

and the Walrus. From there I went through the entire Chip Hilton sports series. By the ninth grade I was reading Charles Dickens and Somerset Maugham and Richard Wright. I was mesmerized by the frankness and rhetorical drama of James Baldwin's essays, though I often missed his allusions.

Reading blessed me with a life that was parallel to the life I was actually living. And all the way through college and graduate school it was this parallel world of reading that most engaged me emotionally and intellectually. School, for me, was never more than counterpoint to the autodidacticism of my actual intellectual engagement.

So, out of childhood despair and without any conscious intention, I developed a parallel self—a rather fearless self that wanted to make its own sense of things. Reading is an encounter with someone else's private and parallel self, and it is impossible to read a lot without wanting to nurture such a self within one's own life. Inevitably, as the years of reading mount, this wildly independent and parallel self wants more and more to express itself in language—that is, to write.

Even as I read constantly, I admitted to no one—least of all myself—that I wanted to "be a writer." Yet in high school I often wrote two weekly essays when only one

❝ In high school I often wrote two weekly essays when only one was required. I sent long and labored letters to the editor of the local newspaper. I wrote love letters for friends. ❞

was required. I sent long and labored letters to the editor of the local newspaper. I wrote love letters for friends to the girls they pined for—any excuse to plunk words down on paper.

So finally it was this parallel life, the fruit of reading, that made writing a necessity for me. My guess is that many writers are born of some crucible, some sharp pinch that sets off the reading and, thus, the parallel life. Maybe we need a second self to buffer us from the first. In any case, this second self becomes more and more urgent over time, less and less repressible. And one writes simply to bring it into reality. ∾

White Guilt and the Western Past

THERE IS SOMETHING RATHER ODD in the way America has come to fight its wars since World War II.

For one thing, it is now unimaginable that we would use anything approaching the full measure of our military power (the nuclear option aside) in the wars we fight. And this seems only reasonable given the relative weakness of our Third World enemies in Vietnam and in the Middle East. But the fact is that we lost in Vietnam, and today, despite our vast power, we are only slogging along—if admirably—in Iraq against a hit-and-run insurgency that cannot stop us even as we seem unable to stop it. Yet no one— including, very likely, the insurgents themselves—believes that America lacks the raw power to defeat this insurgency if it wants to. So clearly it is America that determines the scale of this war. It is America, in fact, that fights so as to make a little room for an insurgency.

Certainly since Vietnam, America has increasingly practiced a policy of minimalism and restraint in war. And now this unacknowledged policy, which always makes a space for the enemy, has us in another long and rather passionless war against a weak enemy.

Why this new minimalism in war?

It began, I believe, in a late-twentieth-century event that transformed the world

> 66 Certainly since Vietnam, America has increasingly practiced a policy of minimalism and restraint in war. 99

more profoundly than the collapse of communism: the world-wide collapse of white supremacy as a source of moral authority, political legitimacy, and even sovereignty. This idea had organized the entire world, divided up its resources, imposed the nation-state system across the globe, and delivered the majority of the world's population into servitude and oppression. After World War II, revolutions across the globe, from India to Algeria and from Indonesia to the American civil rights revolution, defeated the authority inherent in white supremacy, if not the idea itself. And this defeat exacted a price: the West was left stigmatized by its sins. Today, the white West—like Germany after the Nazi defeat—lives in a kind of secular penitence in which the slightest echo of past sins brings down withering condemnation. There is now a cloud over white skin where there once was unquestioned authority.

I call this white guilt not because it is a guilt of conscience but because people stigmatized with moral crimes—here racism and imperialism—lack moral authority and so act guiltily whether they feel guilt or not.

They struggle, above all else, to dissociate themselves from the past sins they are stigmatized with. When they behave in ways that invoke the memory of those sins, they must labor to prove that they have not relapsed into their group's former sinfulness. So when ▸

> " Today, the white West lives in a kind of secular penitence in which the slightest echo of past sins brings down withering condemnation. "

America—the greatest embodiment of Western power—goes to war in Third World Iraq, it must also labor to dissociate that action from the great Western sin of imperialism. Thus, in Iraq we are in two wars, one against an insurgency and another against the past—two fronts, two victories to win, one military, the other a victory of dissociation.

The collapse of white supremacy—and the resulting white guilt—introduced a new mechanism of power into the world: stigmatization with the evil of the Western past. And this stigmatization is power because it affects the terms of legitimacy for Western nations and for their actions in the world. In Iraq, America is fighting as much for the legitimacy of its war effort as for victory in war. In fact, legitimacy may be the more important goal. If a military victory makes us look like an imperialist nation bent on occupying and raping the resources of a poor brown nation, then victory would mean less because it would have no legitimacy. Europe would scorn it. Conversely, if America suffered a military loss in Iraq but in so doing dispelled the imperialist stigma, the loss would be seen as a necessary sacrifice made to restore our nation's legitimacy. Europe's halls of internationalism would suddenly open to us.

Because dissociation from the racist and imperialist stigma is so tied to

66 In Iraq, America is fighting as much for the legitimacy of its war effort as for victory in war. In fact, legitimacy may be the more important goal. 99

legitimacy in this age of white guilt, America's act of going to war can have legitimacy only if it seems to be an act of social work—something that uplifts and transforms the poor brown nation (thus dissociating us from the white exploitations of old). So our war effort in Iraq is shrouded in a new language of social work in which democracy is cast as an instrument of social transformation bringing new institutions, new relations between men and women, new ideas of individual autonomy, new and more open forms of education, new ways of overcoming poverty—war as the Great Society.

This does not mean that President Bush is insincere in his desire to bring democracy to Iraq, nor is it to say that democracy won't ultimately be socially transformative in Iraq. It's just that today the United States cannot go to war in the Third World simply to defeat a dangerous enemy.

White guilt makes our Third World enemies into colored victims, people whose problems—even the tyrannies they live under—were created by the historical disruptions and injustices of the white West. We must "understand" and pity our enemy even as we fight him. And, though Islamic extremism is one of the most pernicious forms of evil opportunism that has ever existed, we have felt compelled to fight it with an almost ▶

managerial minimalism that shows us to be beyond the passions of war—and thus dissociated from the avariciousness of the white supremacist past.

Anti-Americanism, whether in Europe or on the American left, works by the mechanism of white guilt. It stigmatizes America with all the imperialistic and racist ugliness of the white Western past so that America becomes a kind of straw man, a construct of Western sin. (The Abu Ghraib and Guantanamo prisons were the focus of such stigmatization campaigns.) Once the stigma is in place, one need only be anti-American in order to be "good," in order to have an automatic moral legitimacy and power in relation to America. (People as seemingly disparate as President Jacques Chirac and the Reverend Al Sharpton are devoted pursuers of the moral high ground to be found in anti-Americanism.) This formula is the most dependable source of power for today's international left. Virtue and power by mere anti-Americanism. And it is all the more appealing since, unlike real virtues, it requires no sacrifice or effort—only outrage at every slight echo of the imperialist past.

Today words like "power" and "victory" are so stigmatized with Western sin that, in many quarters, it is politically incorrect even to utter them. For the West, "might" can never be right. And victory, when won by the West against a Third World enemy,

❝ Once the stigma is in place, one need only be anti-American in order to be 'good,' in order to have an automatic moral legitimacy and power in relation to America. ❞

is always oppression. But, in reality, military victory is also the victory of one idea and the defeat of another. Only American victory in Iraq defeats the idea of Islamic extremism. But in today's atmosphere of Western contrition, it is impolitic to say so.

America and the broader West are now going through a rather tender era, a time when Western societies have very little defense against the moral accusations that come from their own left wings and from those vast stretches of nonwhite humanity that were once so disregarded.

Europeans are utterly confounded by the swelling Muslim populations in their midst. America has run from its own mounting immigration problem for decades, and even today, after finally taking up the issue, our government seems entirely flummoxed. White guilt is a vacuum of moral authority visited on the present by the shames of the past. In the abstract it seems a slight thing, almost irrelevant, an unconvincing proposition. Yet a society as enormously powerful as America lacks the authority to ask its most brilliant, wealthy, and superbly educated minority students to compete freely for college admission with poor whites who lack all these things. Just can't do it.

Whether the problem is race relations, education, immigration, or war, white guilt imposes so much minimalism and ▶

> " A society as enormously powerful as America lacks the authority to ask its most brilliant, wealthy, and superbly educated minority students to compete freely for college admission with poor whites who lack all these things. "

White Guilt and the Western Past *(continued)*

restraint that our worst problems tend to linger and deepen. Our leaders work within a double bind. If they do what is truly necessary to solve a problem—win a war, fix immigration—they lose legitimacy.

To maintain their legitimacy, they practice the minimalism that makes problems linger. What but minimalism is left when you are running from stigmatization as a "unilateralist cowboy"? And where is the will to truly regulate the southern border when those who ask for this are slimed as bigots? This is how white guilt defines what is possible in America. You go at a problem until you meet stigmatization, then you retreat into minimalism.

Possibly white guilt's worst effect is that it does not permit whites—and nonwhites—to appreciate something extraordinary: the fact that whites in America, and even elsewhere in the West, have achieved a truly remarkable moral transformation. One is forbidden to speak thus, but it is simply true. There are no serious advocates of white supremacy in America today, because whites see this idea as morally repugnant. If there is still the odd white bigot out there surviving past his time, there are millions of whites who only feel good will toward minorities.

This is a fact that must be integrated into our public life—absorbed as new history—so that America can once again feel the moral authority to seriously tackle its most profound problems. Then, if we decide to go to war, it can be with enough ferocity to win.

"White Guilt and the Western Past" appeared in The Wall Street Journal, *May 2, 2006, and is reprinted by permission of the author.* ∾

Have You Read?

From the author of the award-winning
bestseller *The Content of Our Character*
comes a new essay collection that tells the
untold story behind the polarized racial
politics in America today. In *A Dream
Deferred*, Shelby Steele argues that a
second betrayal of black freedom in
the United States—the first one being
segregation—emerged from the
civil rights era when the country
was overtaken by a powerful impulse
to redeem itself from racial shame.
According to Steele, 1960s liberalism
had as its first and all-consuming goal
the expiation of American guilt rather
than the careful development of true
equality between the races. This "culture
of preference" betrayed America's best
principles in order to give whites and
American institutions an iconography
of racial virtue they could use against
the stigma of racial shame. In four
densely argued essays, Steele takes on
the familiar questions of affirmative
action, multiculturalism, diversity,
Afro-centrism, group preferences,
victimization—and what he deems
to be the atavistic powers of race,
ethnicity and gender, the original
causes of oppression. *A Dream
Deferred* is an honest, courageous
look at the perplexing dilemma of

race and democracy in the United States—and what we might do to resolve it.

"The perfect voice of reason in a sea of hate."   —*Los Angeles Times*

"Steele has given eloquent voice to painful truths that are almost always left unspoken in the nation's circumscribed public discourse on race."
                        —*New York Times*

THE CONTENT OF OUR CHARACTER:
A NEW VISION OF RACE IN AMERICA

In this controversial essay collection, Shelby Steele illuminates the origins of the current conflict in race relations—the increase in anger, mistrust, and even violence between blacks and whites. With candor and persuasive argument, he shows us how both black and white Americans have become trapped into seeing color before character, and how social policies designed to lessen racial inequities have instead increased them. *The Content of Our Character* is neither "liberal" nor "conservative," but an honest, courageous look at America's most enduring and wrenching social dilemma.

"One of the best books on race in America to appear in the past twenty-five years. . . . No one who reads it honestly and with an open mind will ever think about race in quite the same way again."
— *Wall Street Journal*

"Steele writes with a rare elegance and honesty. . . . This is one of those rare books that force reexamination of basic assumptions." — *Boston Globe*

Don't miss the next book by your favorite author. Sign up now for AuthorTracker by visiting www.AuthorTracker.com.